A Practitioner's Guide to Digital Platform Business is a must-read for any budding entrepreneur contemplating venturing into a digital platform business. It provides a very practical guide for setting up a platform business, with just the right balance between the business frameworks and real-life case studies. The authors have aptly put together a series of stories of innovative digital startups, from social enterprises to lifestyle, legal services, healthcare, hospitality, and transportation. The book is suitable for practitioners who want to meet the challenges of creating successful businesses in the digital age head-on or for entrepreneurs just wanting to learn about cutting-edge alternative business models.

Professor Bert De Reyck
Dean, Lee Kong Chian School of Business
Singapore Management University

Each of the eight companies contained in this book has a story to tell and the challenges that they face are real. Chiyachantana, Ding, and Hong bring out the best in each story to fit them into a practical and workable framework for practitioners in digital businesses.

Excerpt from the foreword by Shirley Wong
Managing Partner
TNF Ventures Pte Ltd
and
Entrepreneur-in-Residence,
SMU Institute of Innovation & Entrepreneurship

Every forward-thinking startup today understands the power of building platforms that achieve network effects. This book innovates on the popular and familiar Business Model Canvas to help startups design their businesses as platforms right from the start, and shows how to apply it through real-world case studies.

Victor Ng
Chief Product Officer
Fundnel

A Practitioner's Guide to
Digital Platform Business

A Practitioner's Guide to
Digital Platform Business

Chiraphol N Chiyachantana
David K Ding
Jack J Hong

Singapore Management University, Singapore

World Scientific

NEW JERSEY · LONDON · SINGAPORE · BEIJING · SHANGHAI · HONG KONG · TAIPEI · CHENNAI · TOKYO

Published by

World Scientific Publishing Co. Pte. Ltd.
5 Toh Tuck Link, Singapore 596224
USA office: 27 Warren Street, Suite 401-402, Hackensack, NJ 07601
UK office: 57 Shelton Street, Covent Garden, London WC2H 9HE

Library of Congress Cataloging-in-Publication Data
Names: Chiyachantana, Chiraphol N., author. |
    Ding, David K., 1959–   author. | Hong, Jack J., author.
Title: A practitioner's guide to digital platform business /
    Chiraphol N Chiyachantana, David K Ding, Jack J Hong.
Description: Hackensack, NJ : World Scientific, [2022] | Includes index.
Identifiers: LCCN 2021059130 | ISBN 9789811253263 (hardcover) |
    ISBN 9789811253270 (ebook) | ISBN 9789811253287 (ebook other)
Subjects: LCSH: Electronic commerce--Singapore--Case studies. |
    New business enterprises--Computer networks--Singapore--Case studies. |
    New business enterprises--Singapore--Management--Case studies. |
    Business enterprises--Technological innovations--Singapore--Case studies.
Classification: LCC HF5548.325.S55 C45 2022 | DDC 658.8/72095957--dc23/eng/20220111
LC record available at https://lccn.loc.gov/2021059130

British Library Cataloguing-in-Publication Data
A catalogue record for this book is available from the British Library.

For any available supplementary material, please visit
https://www.worldscientific.com/worldscibooks/10.1142/12754#t=suppl

Desk Editor: Nicole Ong

Typeset by Stallion Press
Email: enquiries@stallionpress.com

About the Authors

Dr. Chiraphol New Chiyachantana is Assistant Professor of Finance (Education) at the Singapore Management University. His teaching and research interests lie primarily in Business Models and Innovation, Asset Pricing and Capital Markets, Financial Innovations and FinTech, and Entrepreneurial Finance. He has published his research in leading journals such as *the Journal of Finance, Journal of Financial and Quantitative Analysis, Journal of Banking and Finance, Journal of Financial Markets and Journal of Financial Research.*

He consistently ranks in the top percentile in teaching effectiveness and has won 14 teaching awards — the Dean's Teaching Honors and the University-Wide Teaching Excellence Award in 2007.

Dr. David Ding is Associate Professor of Finance (Education) and Director of the CFA University Affiliation Program at the Singapore Management University, where he had served as Director of the Master of Applied Finance (China) program. Prior to SMU, he was the Foundation Professor of Finance and coordinator of the Finance program at the University of New South Wales (Asia) and was a faculty member and director of a research center at the Nanyang Business School, Nanyang Technological University. He had also held appointments as Professor of Finance and Associate Head of School at Massey University, New Zealand. His research interests are in market microstructure, emerging markets, corporate governance, corporate social responsibility, and sustainability. Before joining academia, he worked in commercial banking and management consulting. He was President of the Asian Finance Association, President of the Pacific Basin Financial Management Society, and served on the panel of experts on securities offences at the Commercial Affairs Department of the Singapore Police Force. He is a member of the American Finance Association, Financial Management Association International, Asian Finance Association, CFA Institute, and the Asian Shadow Financial Regulatory Committee.

Dr. Jack Hong is an expert in end-to-end Artificial Intelligence (AI) applications. He is currently the Data Science advisor to Vertex Holdings and AI advisor to Certis Group's Centre for Applied Intelligence. Dr. Hong creates proprietary business capabilities in these roles using cutting-edge research and engineering skillsets to deliver artificial super-intelligence in use-cases involving natural language programming, computer vision, and analytics. He also leads Research Room Pte Ltd, an AI consulting outfit that delivers complex decision-making solutions for large organizations, and Integrum Pte Ltd, the developer of Kailash, a microservices orchestration platform that delivers AI and Data as a service.

Dr. Hong is an adjunct faculty with the Singapore Management University (SMU) and has been actively teaching undergraduate and postgraduate programs (Digital transformation, python programming, data science, and financial economics) since 2014. In addition to his SMU commitments, Dr. Hong trains professionals and aspiring interns in AI capabilities, from theoretical foundations to engineering know-hows, in his day-to-day roles.

Dr. Hong's research interests lie in developing new deep learning models that can solve challenging business problems. He has extensive commercial and civil service experience before earning his Ph.D. in Finance from the Singapore Management University.

Acknowledgements

Over a casual lunch at Funan Center in Downtown Singapore, in February 2021, New discussed his idea of writing a book together with David. But on what topic? New was into fintech and entrepreneurship and David, corporate social responsibility and sustainability. The COVID-19 pandemic was into its second year and businesses continue to be disrupted. What kinds of businesses can survive during such uncertain times? The two of us put our heads together and brainstormed, and eventually zeroed down to businesses that can transform themselves digitally to meet the challenges of the day. But neither could claim to be experts in digital business.

Jack, who runs a consulting outfit, and who is an expert in end-to-end Artificial Intelligence (AI) applications and teaches digital transformation at SMU, is an ideal partner. Over another lunch, Jack readily accepted New and David's invitation to co-author a book on digital businesses, particularly those that utilize a platform business model to drive their entire value chain. Thus, *A Practitioner's Guide to Digital Platform Business* was born.

This book would not have been possible without the relentless support of the eight *can-do* startups that form the backdrop of our studies on their digital journey. Their utter willingness to share their stories, with totally unselfish motives, allow other likeminded budding entrepreneurs an unparalleled opportunity to learn important lessons on the key drivers of their success and contributors to the challenges that they face. We truly appreciate the time they afforded us through several meetings and interviews. We have included their individual stories on the challenges and opportunities that they face during the Covid-19 pandemic, giving special insight into how they overcome challenges and grasp unique opportunities during uncertain times.

We started off by engaging the co-founders of each startup firm through a consulting project run by two classes of our MBA students. We are grateful to our very capable and hardworking MBA cohort of January 2021. Each MBA team was assigned one startup to work with — from understanding their business model and challenges, to making workable recommendations for the startup's consideration. The experience and feedback from the startups have largely been very positive.

SMU's business librarian, Ms. Lim Hwee Min, was particularly helpful in providing a specially arranged training session to the MBA students on the relevant sources of information and databases. This was valuable in arming them with the relevant industry background information prior to their meetings with the co-founders of the startups.

SMU's *Institute of Innovation and Entrepreneurship* (IIE) has been instrumental in helping us identify suitable startups that we could work with. We very much appreciate the many hours of hard work put in by especially Jinzhou Yi and Alvin Tam, two senior managers at IIE. Without their help in making the connections and providing background information of the startups, we wouldn't have been able to come this far in such a short time. We owe them our heartfelt gratitude.

We acknowledge and appreciate our reviewers, Professor Bert De Reyck, Dean of the Lee Kong Chian School of Business at SMU, and Victor Ng, Chief Product Officer at Fundnel, for their generous comments, constructive feedback, and strong encouragement.

We thank Ms. Shirley Wong, Entrepreneur-in-Residence at SMU's IIE and Managing Partner at TNF Ventures Pte Ltd, for writing the Foreword. Her words are particularly inspiring and uplifting.

Mitchell Simpson, our research assistant during the earlier part of the project, was very helpful in communicating with the startups and in collating and sorting out the materials for the book.

Nicole Ong, our editor from World Scientific Publishing, was always patient and accommodating to our many demands. We very much appreciate her helpful comments and suggestions toward the speedy completion of the book.

Last, but not least, we wish to thank our family and friends for their encouragement and support during our book-writing journey. We hope you will enjoy reading about the individual stories of the budding startups contained in this book and lend your support to them when the opportunity arises.

Foreword

In any kind of enterprise, interruption to its way of doing business is a given. However, the myriad disruptions caused by the COVID-19 pandemic starting from early 2020 is unprecedented and has impacted almost all businesses, be they large or small, physical, or virtual. Those that survive are able to seize the opportunities that have presented themselves and twitched their business models to take advantage of newer ways of doing business. They dare to embrace new technologies and take on calculated risks. They are not afraid to try out new business models so long as they can see how their costs can be controlled in a sustainable manner.

Digital businesses are among the biggest disruptors to mainstream traditional companies. Some started prior to the pandemic and may be struggling to survive, but the pandemic gave them an unexpected push with wider opportunities and markets. Avenues that seemed unfeasible suddenly became viable due to changing consumer attitudes brought about by the pandemic. Yet others started during the pandemic or because of the pandemic. The resulting impetus opened new revenue streams to them when customers and consumers became more willing to try out new ways of purchasing and are open to alternative consumption models.

In their book, *A Practitioner's Guide to Digital Platform Business*, Chiyachantana, Ding, and Hong have very aptly highlighted several recently formed digital businesses on their journey toward running a successful platform business, the challenges that they face, and the opportunities that they are able to harness during the COVID-19 pandemic. These budding enterprises straddle across multifarious industries — from legal services to hospitality, transportation to life-style, and healthcare to social enterprises. There is something for anyone who is interested in (i) the latest developments in these industries during the digital era, (ii) important considerations in starting a digital business, and (iii) pitfalls to avoid when running a platform business.

As an entrepreneur and having spent more than 28 years in the IT and technology industry in various management roles, I have mentored startups and helped them secure funding, access to resources, and make connections in the market. I have witnessed those that have succeeded (and failed) and shared in their joys and sorrows. Very often, those that fail and are not afraid to pick them-selves up to try again to grow stronger, and not repeat their past mistakes. This book contains many examples of personal stories of young entrepreneurs with their never-say-die attitude, how they got started, their ever-evolving business model, their revenue and cost structure, and the multitude of challenges and opportunities that they face, including those amid the COVID-19 pandemic.

Each of the eight companies contained in this book has a story to tell and the challenges that they face are real. Chiyachantana, Ding, and Hong bring out the best in each story to fit them into a practical and workable framework for practitioners in digital busi-nesses. They balance their framework with real-life case studies to provide both current and aspiring practitioners "with the tools for creating successful businesses in the digital age, while at the same time serving as a cautionary tale for those who value businesses by the technology they wield and not the strategies they execute."

Shirley Wong
Managing Partner
TNF Ventures Pte Ltd
and
Entrepreneur-in-Residence,
SMU Institute of Innovation & Entrepreneurship

Contents

Introduction

What Happened in the Last Decade?

This is a rhetorical question. The business landscape in the last decade was surreal — exhilaration, fear, opportunities, and threats all rolled into one messy landscape. Business leaders are accustomed to seeing disruptions. They know that new opportunities avail whenever a deck of cards gets re-shuffled. Many were ready to pounce, but most end up defeated. Never had the world seen disruptions of such unprecedented speed, scope, and scale. Business leaders never anticipated that most disruptive businesses used digital strategies and a small talent pool to sidestep the traditional competencies that mega-corporations needed decades to build with legions of employees.

To put this into perspective, the largest 500 corporations on the New Stock Exchange collectively grew three times from 2010 to 2012. The information technology segment of this group grew eight times in the same period.[1] The growth rate of digital vs. non-digital companies is not only worlds apart; it feels as though they are operating in different eras. As a further blow to the ego of business veterans, most of these digital disruptors are not incumbents but rather outsiders to the industry that they had disrupted. The founders of Airbnb, Uber, Netflix, and Spotify had two things in common:

---

[1] We compared the values of the SPDR Technology Select ETF index against the S&P 500 index between 2010 and 2021.

they understood digital technology and had no experience in the industries that they disrupted.

We are straddling between two eras

The world is in a transition state between the third and fourth Industrial Revolutions (IR) (Table 1). The defining technology towards the end of the third IR is the Internet and Cloud Computing, which underpins the core offerings of many tech giants today, from the e-commerce and cloud infrastructure platforms of Alibaba and Amazon to the booking platforms of Airbnb and Uber.

This technology blurred the divide between economic activities in the physical and virtual space, an experience that we associate with the coming of the fourth IR. Alibaba's massive ecosystem of e-commerce platforms, physical supermarkets, supply chains, delivery networks, payment systems, and wealth management is a good example.

According to the Flexera 2021 State of the Cloud Report, cloud computing for businesses has become ubiquitous, with 99% of all

Table 1:   Timelines and representative technologies of Industrial Revolutions

Era	Period	
1st Industrial Revolution	1760–1840	• Mechanized production using power produced through water and steam. (e.g., Britain's textile industry)
2nd Industrial Revolution	Late 19th to 20th century	• Electricity powering mass production • Internal combustion engines revolutionizing transportation • Telecommunications reducing information distances
3rd Industrial Revolution	1970–Present	• Economic activities supported by Electronics, Computing, and Information Technology • Internet and Cloud Computing (1977– Present)
Industrial Revolution 3.5		
4th Industrial Revolution	2010–Present	• Industrial applications that fuse the digital and physical spaces • Robotics, Internet-of-things, blockchains, edge, and new computing paradigms leading to Artificial General Intelligence

respondents using some form of it compared to 72% in 2016. However, McKinsey's Global Survey on the State of AI in 2020 reports that less than 25% of today's business use-cases adopt some form of Artificial Intelligence. Thus, the world is still transitioning between the third and fourth IRs, and opportunities abound for innovators and disruptors.

Disruption: Technology or Strategy?

Digital technology is not something new. The Internet was born on 1 January 1983 and became commercially available around the globe in the 1990s. The rise of internet-based businesses built on data and computing resources was not smooth sailing. Many investors were spooked and burned during the dot com bubble, where money flooded into these start-ups fueled by unreasonable optimism. Investors lost trillions of dollars when the bubble burst around 2000 to 2002, and massive layoffs in the technology field followed suit.

If we examine the core technologies that power the businesses of today's digital giants: they still revolve around the Internet, data, and computing resources, albeit stronger versions of it. Thus, technological advancements cannot fully explain the sudden disruptions caused by digital businesses from 2010 onwards.

If technology is not the answer, it must be how digital businesses use it that makes a difference. This realization is excellent news for the rest of us who know Python as a snake and not the programming language. At the same time, this is a cautionary tale for those who value businesses by the technology they wield and not the strategies that they execute.

What is this Book About, and Who is it For?

This book is a practitioner's guide to digital business models, and our target audiences are entrepreneurs, MBA and upper-level undergraduate students, and business executives. With a set of simple-to-understand frameworks distilled into an easy-to-use model canvas and real-life case studies, this book provides business students and practitioners with the tools to create successful businesses in the digital age.

Chapter 1 discusses the core frameworks that have defined digital disruptors' success and provides practitioners with an easy-to-use platform business canvas. In each of the following chapters, we share valuable experience, insights, and analysis of eight early Singapore start-ups. They are:

- **Lexagle** — Soaring Above
- **RushOwl** — A Route for Everyone
- **Trabble** — Changing the Way We Travel
- **Savour!** — Savouring with Savour!
- **ThriftCity** — A Smarter Way to Shop
- **Friday.AI** — Advancing One Friday At A Time)
- **Kura Kura** — The Lovable Kura
- **Drive Ride Buddy** — A Digital Journey

We hope that our readers will be inspired by these ideas and draw comfort from knowing that they can use a set of frameworks and tools to create the next disruptive platform business. Happy reading!

Chapter 1

Platform Business Model

How have Business Strategies Changed in the Digital Era?

We can break down a business' digital life cycle into three phases as seen in Table 1: digitization, digitalization, and digital transformation.

Today, most companies in developed countries have digitized their data and adopted digitalization to improve their working processes. A common mistake that companies make is to treat digital technology as nothing more than a replacement for traditional business processes. The results are often disappointing — high implementation costs, long delays, confusing process transitions, discrepancies between promised and delivered products, failed change management, and little revenue upside to show. Instead, successful innovators focus on creating new competitive advantages with digital technology while re-organizing their resources to deliver new value propositions. This is the core mindset behind digital transformation.

> "The form of organization that survives in an activity is the one that delivers the product demanded by customers at the lowest price while covering costs."
>
> — Fama and Jensen, 1998

Table 1: Three stages of a business' digital lifecycle

Digitization	Digitalization	Digital Transformation
Businesses adopt technology that transforms and stores analog data in digital formats that are easier to retrieve, process, and analyze.	Businesses adopt technology that allows users to complete social, professional, and economic activities via digital tools.	Businesses derive new competitive advantages by re-organizing their resources around digital technology.
E.g., Vinyl records and tapes to Compact Discs (CDs) and Digital Versatile Discs (DVDs)	E.g., Electronic contracts and e-payment systems.	E.g., e-commerce platforms.

For a business to be successful, it must deliver products and services that customers demand. Most, if not all entrepreneurs do not argue against this wisdom. However, few genuinely internalize it in their corporate strategy. The great Steve Jobs acknowledged this as one of his early failings in an interview in 1997: *"... you've got to start with the customer experience and work backward for the technology. You can't start with the technology and try to figure out where you're going to try to sell it. And I made this mistake probably more than anybody else in this room."*

Digitization and digitalization have shifted the power of decision-making from businesses to consumers. Information, opinions, reviews, and complaints are easily crowd-sourced from social media. Information barriers are practically non-existent, and influencing public opinion is cheap, fast, and accessible today — the results: louder and immediate voices for better product-market fits, low switching costs, and winner-takes-all.

In response to increasingly powerful consumers, the priority of business thinking must change from an economies of scale cost perspective to a customer value proposition-based one. This change in priority will cause a cascading effect that shifts competitive advantages from traditional business strategies to new digital-based ones.

In *The Digital Playbook* by David Rogers, Columbia Business School, the author highlights changes to five business strategies that define

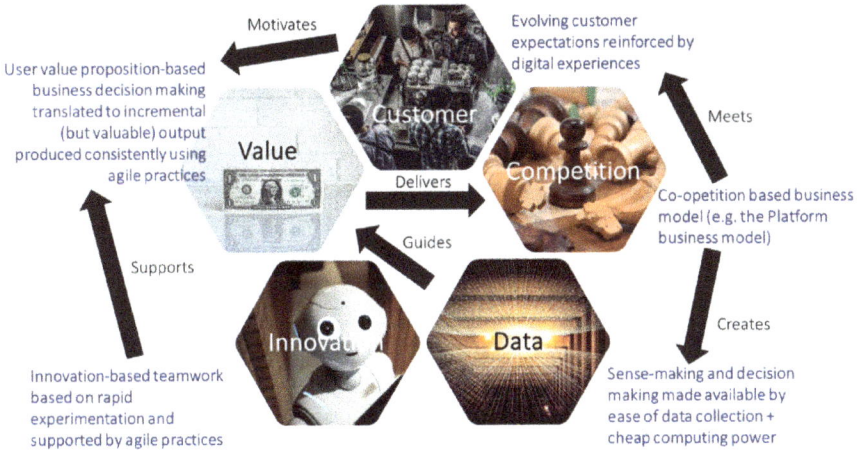

Figure 1:   The relationship between the five domains of strategies

companies' competitive advantages in the new digital age. These are the **Customer**, **Competition**, **Data**, **Innovation**, and **Value**. In Figure 1, we build on David Rogers' insights and explain the relationship between these five domains from an entrepreneur's standpoint.

User Value Proposition. Customer expectations now lead business strategies. Instead of starting with "what the business can do", corporations must first answer, "what do my customers want?". This starting point is the crux of user value proposition-based thinking. Two modern product development styles, agile and design thinking, starts from defining and refining user value propositions.

Architect the Competition. Today's customers have a clear definition of acceptable digital experiences. They want engaging content, personalization, to be heard, and to connect with everyone else. And they want it anytime, anywhere, now. For a new corporation, getting every element correct "now" is next to impossible. Thus, businesses need to rethink how they perceive competition: from a zero-sum game to a co-opetition-based partnership. In the latter, partners work together to expand the economic pie, either through a larger market share or by disrupting other industries. We call this co-opetition-based business model a platform when it is still in its initial stages of growth. When the platform scales, it typically becomes an ecosystem. The remaining sections in this chapter are devoted to understanding how to design such a business model.

Augment Intelligence with Data. The definition of a business ecosystem is one where end-to-end transactions between producers and consumers take place within the confines of its walls. These data are privy to the orchestrator of the business, allowing them to understand individual customer behavior and needs. In marketing, we often segment customers into broad categories. With the help of machine learning models, we can target individuals according to what makes them tick. This ability is known as personalization.

Drive Changes with Innovation. As businesses become more dynamic at meeting customer needs, customer preferences will change rapidly as a result. For companies to maintain their competitive advantage, they need to evolve their products and services as rapidly as possible. Traditional linear management techniques emphasize quality through standardizing deliverables with multiple layers of reporting and approvals. This hierarchical approach results in a situation where market decisions are made by the people who are furthest away from the ground. In ecosystems, evolution (not management) is the mechanism that the fittest uses to survive. When applied to a corporation, evolution comes from innovation, and success is defined by how many experiments we can squeeze into a given amount of time. This concept is known as rapid experimentation. Today, many successful companies have changed their management style from a hierarchy-based to an agile-based one to encourage rapid experimentation and create products and services that are more closely fitted to their customers' needs.

From Linear Business Models to Platforms and Ecosystems

The traditional business model canvas (BMC) is linear (Figure 2), with upstream producers on the left (under Key Partners) and downstream consumers (under Customers) on the right. Many users of the BMC inherently assume that the company is a middleman that makes profit margins by procuring from the supply side, adding some value in the middle, and selling the output to the demand side.

This thinking accurately represents most business models in the third IR, where economies of scale, barriers to entry, and power over suppliers and customers are critical drivers of profitability. With the shift towards the changes in the five business strategies outlined in

Key Partners	Key Activities	Value Propositions	Customer Relationships	Customer Segments
Who are your most important partners and suppliers? What are the key activities and resources we need from them?	What key activities do we need to do in support of our value propositions?	What value do we deliver to the customers? What pain points are we trying to solve?	What type of relationship do we want to establish with each of the customer segments?	Which customer segments are we creating value propositions for?
	Key Resources What key resources do we need to do in support of our value propositions?	What are we offering to each customer segment?	**Channels** What channels are we using to reach our customer segments? How are we using each channel?	
Cost Structure What are the key cost drivers of this business mode?		**Revenue Streams** What value and how much are our customers willing to pay for it?		

Figure 2:   Basic Business Model Canvas

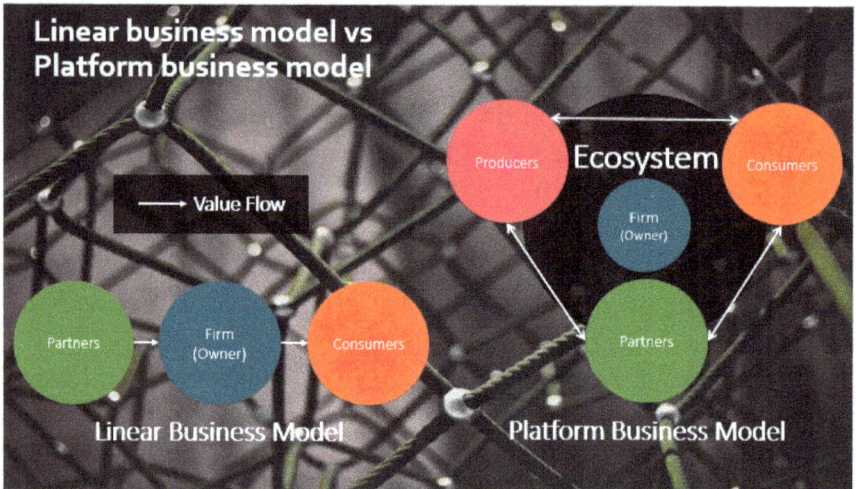

Figure 3:   Linear vs. Platform Business Model

the previous section, these core competencies no longer hold for business models designed around co-opetition.

In a traditionally linear business model, the consumers of a firm interact only with the firm, and they rarely know who the suppliers are. In a platform business model, producers (***we term any suppliers or merchants of products and services as producers***) and partners directly interact with the consumers within the firm's safe, trusting, and productive environment (Figure 3). The latter is a robust design that sidesteps many of the strategic competencies of a traditional firm:

1. Demand and supply can dynamically and rapidly adjust towards equilibrium. Consumers can quickly reveal their needs and expectations through the platform. It is in the incentive of a community of producers to provide products and services to meet these needs. The firm is no longer responsible for guessing and keeping up with rapidly changing consumer needs.

2. Barriers to entry are no longer about secrecy. The value of the firm as a platform orchestrator is clear. First, transactions between producers and consumers will not happen without this safe and trusting environment. Second, producers can focus on what they do well — respond rapidly to changing consumer needs while relying on the platform's transactional functions such as ordering, feedback, delivery, and payments.

3. Partners play a critical role in helping the firm facilitate transactional functions that require high expertise or capital expenditure, such as electronic payments and last-mile delivery.

4. The firm owns a high volume of transaction data, which reveals highly personal information about participating producers, consumers, and partners. Using analytics and machine learning algorithms, the firm can extract insights at a larger scale, wider scope, faster speed, and sharper precision compared to before, leading to new competitive advantages such as personalization.

5. The firm, now asset-light, can focus its attention and resources on expanding the ecosystem by creating more platforms, including some that may disrupt other industries. We have seen many such examples, from Carousell as a peer-to-peer 2nd hand flea market to facilitating transactions of collector's items and pre-owned vehicles, to Grab becoming a digital bank from a ride-hailing business.

A platform views producers, consumers, and partners as **customers** and aligns their incentives with the firm through transparency. Every player bears the direct consequences, costs, and benefits of their actions. Positive interactions within and between customer types create network effects that pull more customers into the platform and make it hard to leave:

1. More producers mean that consumers can procure various needs without leaving the platform, hence being able to attract

more consumers. This case of one customer type drawing more users from the other types is an **indirect network effect**.

2. More consumers will result in more sales trends, ratings, and reviews, thus attracting more consumers. This case of one customer type drawing more users from the same type is a **direct network effect**.

3. More partners mean more functionalities that can facilitate transactions even more smoothly and conveniently.

Network effects are powerful and disruptive in platform businesses because they create **high-density multi-source networks** by pulling various customer types into the platform. Communications within the networks of traditional companies primarily originate from a single source and are either uni-directional (pre-social media days) or bi-directional (post-social media days). There are conventional business networks like consortiums or buying groups. However, the density of these exclusive networks is still too low to create the disruptive network effects that we see in platform businesses today.

Last but not least, understanding the economics of network effects requires a mindset shift. Most traditional businesses build their business strategies on economies of scale where they increase profit margins by reducing costs. Network effects do not reduce costs, but they increase profit margins by increasing revenue through scale.

The Platform Business Model Canvas

We extend the basic business model canvas to cover the essential components of a platform business model, as shown in Figure 4, and detail the steps to use this tool in the following pages.

Step 1: Create your Core Value Propositions.

Platform Business Model Canvas

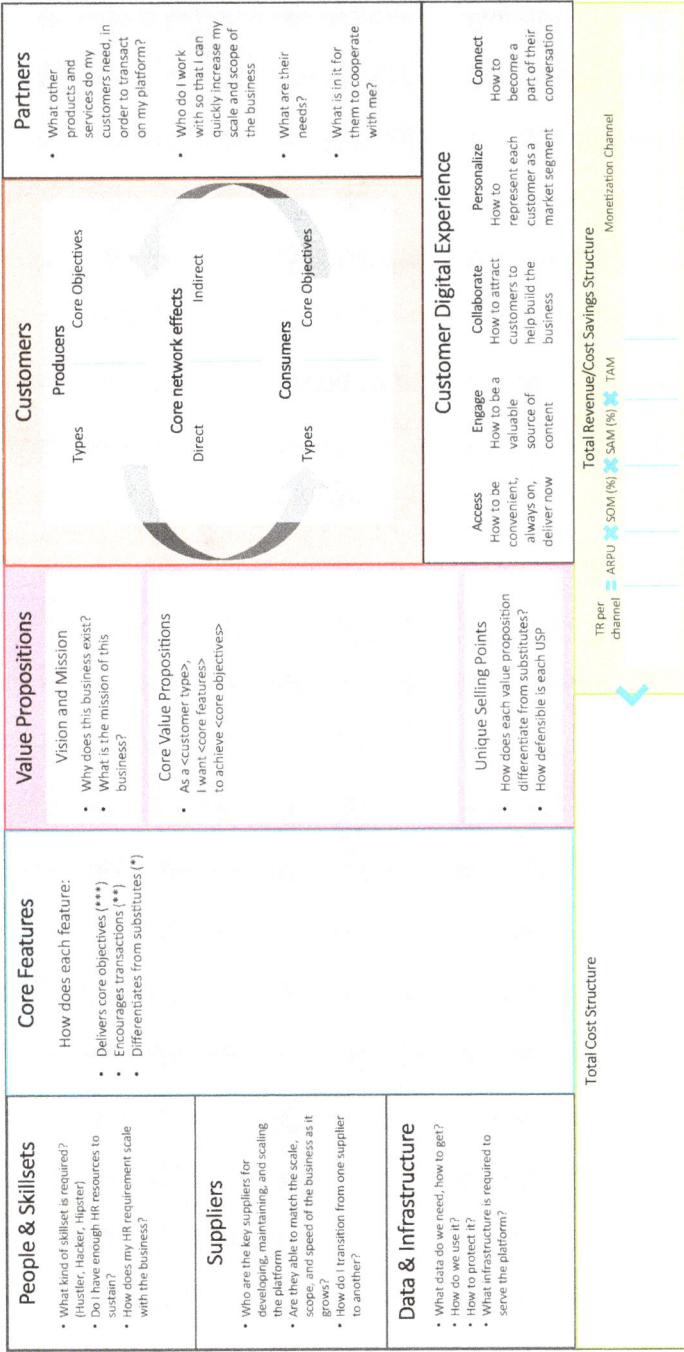

Figure 4: Platform Business Model Canvas

People & Skillsets

- What kind of skillset is required? (Hustler, Hacker, Hipster)
- Do I have enough HR resources to sustain?
- How does my HR requirement scale with the business?

Suppliers

- Who are the key suppliers for developing, maintaining, and scaling the platform
- Are they able to match the scale, scope, and speed of the business as it grows?
- How do I transition from one supplier to another?

Data & Infrastructure

- What data do we need, how to get?
- How do we use it?
- How to protect it?
- What infrastructure is required to serve the platform?

Core Features

How does each feature:

- Delivers core objectives (***)
- Encourages transactions (**)
- Differentiates from substitutes (*)

Value Propositions

Vision and Mission
- Why does this business exist?
- What is the mission of this business?

Core Value Propositions
As a <customer type>,
I want <core features>
to achieve <core objectives>

Unique Selling Points
- How does each value proposition differentiate from substitutes?
- How defensible is each USP

Customers

Producers
Types   Core Objectives

Core network effects
Direct   Indirect

Consumers
Types   Core Objectives

Partners

- What other products and services do my customers need, in order to transact on my platform?
- Who do I work with so that I can quickly increase my scale and scope of the business
- What are their needs?
- What is in it for them to cooperate with me?

Customer Digital Experience

Access How to be convenient, always on, deliver now

Engage How to be a valuable source of content

Collaborate How to attract customers to help build the business

Personalize How to represent each customer as a market segment

Connect How to become a part of their conversation

Total Revenue/Cost Savings Structure
Monetization Channel

TR per channel = ARPU ✕ SOM (%) ✕ SAM (%) ✕ TAM

TR = Total revenue
ARPU = Average revenue per user
SOM: Serviceable obtainable market   TAM: Total available market
SAM: Serviceable available market

Total Cost Structure

Value Propositions
Vision and Mission
• Why does this business exist?
• What is the mission of this business?
Core Value Propositions
• As a <customer type>, I want <core features> to achieve <core objectives>
Unique Selling Points
• How does each value proposition differentiate from substitutes?
• How defensible is each USP

Conceive value propositions from the perspective of customer needs. We have provided a helpful templated statement to define value propositions:

"As a <customer type>, I want what <features> to achieve which <objectives>."

From a producer's perspective, an example of a value proposition may look like this: As a merchant, I want an order tracking service that combines and forwards bulk delivery orders to chosen providers to save on costs.

From a consumer's perspective, an example of a value proposition may look like this: As a buyer, I want to see prices and reviews of similar items across multiple e-commerce platforms to ensure that I get the best deals.

As a platform orchestrator, you may also want to identify the unique selling points of your core value propositions by how well it differentiates from existing substitutes.

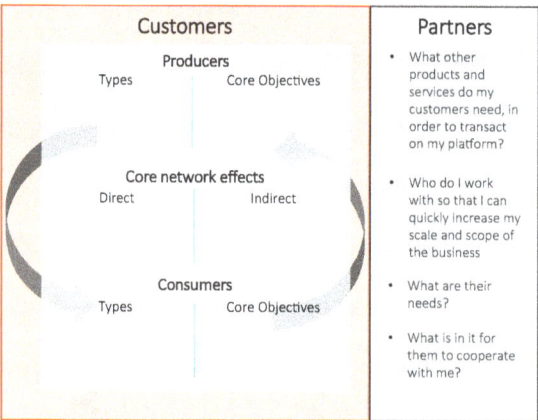

Customers	Partners
Producers — Types, Core Objectives	• What other products and services do my customers need, in order to transact on my platform?
Core network effects — Direct, Indirect	• Who do I work with so that I can quickly increase my scale and scope of the business
Consumers — Types, Core Objectives	• What are their needs?
	• What is in it for them to cooperate with me?

Step 2: Identify your target audiences within each customer type and their network effects.

Producers are customers of the platform that provides goods and services directly to consumers within the platform.

Partners participate in the platform by providing services to facilitate the transactions between producers and consumers.

Network effects are created when the increase of one customer type affects the platform's value for the same or different customer types. Readers need to be mindful that not all network effects are positive. Congestion and crowding out are the most common adverse network effects that disincentivize producers and consumers from using the platform.

Customer Digital Experience				
Access	Engage	Collaborate	Personalize	Connect
How to be convenient, always on, deliver now	How to be a valuable source of content	How to attract customers to help build the business	How to represent each customer as a market segment	How to become a part of their conversation

Step 3: Network effects in digital platforms are driven by the following five areas of digital experiences. Ensure that your solution contains as many of them as possible.

1. **Accessibility**. Accessibility is not just about users being able to use the platform anytime, anywhere. A user journey that requires many steps to create an account make a decision, complete a transaction, or require pre-requisite skillsets or knowledge, will also affect the willingness of customers to use it.

2. **Engagement**. Platform orchestrators should provide valuable information that will make customers want to visit and stay on the website. Engagement value is driven more by the relevancy of the content than the form of delivery. For example, corporate videos may not be as relevant as product reviews for some platform businesses. Rather than having a corporate video feature, it will be more beneficial to encourage producers and consumers to upload video reviews.

3. **Opportunities for collaboration**. For some types of platform businesses, there are opportunities for consumers to become producers quickly. A good example is Carousell, a used-goods marketplace where anyone can sell new and used products and services.

4. **Personalization**. Personalization is not about having unique individual accounts or allowing users to customize what they see on the platform. Platform orchestrators need to treat personalization in the same way that they think about market segmentation, except that personalization is in segments of one user each. The business objective is to encourage more transactions by helping users discover new needs and facilitate better and faster decision-making.

5. **Connection**. Sowing a seed of information is not hard. However, if we do not water it continuously, the plant will wither and die. Connections within networks behave the same, and platform orchestrators need to shape their growth by being a part of it. Depending on the type of platform businesses, connections can be conversations, user interactions, or user journeys. The objective is to make users feel that they belong in the platform, together with the orchestrator and other customers.

Core Features

How does each feature:

- Delivers core objectives (***)
- Encourages transactions (**)
- Differentiates from substitutes (*)

Step 4: List down the core features required to deliver the value propositions, unique selling points, and digital experiences.

People & Skillsets

- What kind of skillset is required? (Hustler, Hacker, Hipster)
- Do I have enough HR resources to sustain?
- How does my HR requirement scale with the business?

Step 5: List the essential cost drivers required to develop and deliver the necessary core features of the platform. These include human resources and skillsets, data and infrastructure, as well as suppliers. Suppliers are differentiated from producers and partners because they supply products and services to the business and not directly with customers. Some examples are cloud services and storage centers.

Suppliers

- Who are the key suppliers for developing, maintaining, and scaling the platform
- Are they able to match the scale, scope, and speed of the business as it grows?
- How do I transition from one supplier to another?

Data & Infrastructure

- What data do we need, how to get?
- How do we use it?
- How to protect it?
- What infrastructure is required to serve the platform?

Total Cost Structure

Total Revenue/Cost Savings Structure

TR per channel = ARPU ✕ SOM (%) ✕ SAM (%) ✕ TAM   Monetization Channel

TR = Total revenue   SOM: Serviceable obtainable market   TAM: Total available market
ARPU = Average revenue per user   SAM: Serviceable available market

Step 6: List down the estimated value of the revenue and cost structures at maturity. These values should be a translation of the revenue and cost drivers of the business model created in steps one to five. Revenue may be harder to estimate, so we have provided a reference formula as follows:

> **Total revenue per monetization channel =**
> **Total Addressable Market (TAM) × Serviceable Available Market (SAM %) × Serviceable Obtainable Market (SOM %) × Average revenue per user/unit (ARPU $)**

The following is one interpretation of the above formula that we can use from the standpoint of a digital platform business:

1. TAM refers to the total number of users in a market that may need the proposed value propositions of a specific monetization channel.
2. SAM refers to the percentage of TAM that is willing to transact for these value propositions.
3. SOM refers to the percentage of SAM that the platform business can acquire.
4. ARPU refers to the estimated revenue per user/unit.

The following are two scenarios for reference, with values for demonstration purposes only.

Scenario 1: A content platform that publishes articles featuring food from F&B locations around Singapore

Monetization channel: Subscription-only access to the platform priced at S$9.99 per month

TAM = Total number of people in Singapore that may use the content to make a dining decision

= Singapore's resident population aged between 10 to 89
~5m

SAM = Percentage of TAM that is willing to pay the subscription fee
       = 0
SOM = 0
ARPU per year = S$9.99 × 12 = S$119.88
Total revenue per year for this monetization channel = S$119.88 × 0 = S$ 0

Scenario 2: A platform that matches producers of home-cook food with consumers within a neighborhood

Monetization channel: Take 15% commissions from producers on transacted selling price

TAM = Total number of working adults in Singapore
      ~4m

SAM = Percentage of TAM that order takeaways/deliveries at least once a week
      = 25%
      = 1m

SOM = Percentage of SAM that the platform can acquire
      = 1%
      – 10,000

ARPU per year = Average order value × number of orders per month × 12 months × commissions rate
                = S$20 × 4 × 12 months × 15%
                = S$144

Total revenue per year for this monetization channel = S$144 × 10,000 = S$ 1,440,000

Congratulations, you are now ready to design a platform business model with the essential components for success. In the following chapters, we will analyze and share lessons from eight digital start-ups from Singapore.

Chapter 2

Lexagle (Soaring Above)

Introduction

There has been a rise in the demand for Contract Lifecycle Management (CLM) to identify loopholes from past contracts, reduce organization penalties from non-compliant practices, and streamline decision-making processes involving the cross-referencing of past agreements. In addition, CLM can help organizations easily partner with other firms to expand their consumer bases. Consequently, the demand for CLM software in both public and private sectors, in industries ranging from financial services, healthcare to manufacturing, remains high.[1]

With a mission to solve one of business managers' perplexing mysteries of '*where are all my contracts?*' (Gerald Heng) and '*why are there no common tech platforms for lawyers?*' (Jimmy Tan), the two co-founders set out to address these challenges by creating Lexagle. Lexagle is the first AI-driven Contract Lifecycle Management platform in Singapore. The platform aims to resolve the pain of managing the lifecycle of contracts, from the contracts' drafting to the storage and retrieval of past agreements, which can be a ticking time bomb if not correctly handled. Businesses tend to overlook this fact, as they often view it as a non-revenue generating

---

[1] IMARC Group, 2021. https://www.researchandmarkets.com/reports/5264072/contract-lifecycle-management-software-market

activity and are unwilling to invest further in a better contract management system. Lexagle provides a centralized repository for contract management, allowing businesses to mitigate future chaos in locating past contracts. Lexagle provides auto-generated templates, digital signatures, managing key dates stated within contract clauses, and reminding firms of their contractual obligations to reduce the cost of damages or lost opportunities from canceled contracts. Today, Lexagle digitizes the entire contracting process from start to finish, simplifying the whole Contract Lifecycle Management process.

The Founders

Gerald Heng, Jimmy Tan, and Fayanne King co-founded Lexagle in 2019. Gerald spent the first ten years of his career as a corporate M&A lawyer before joining a FinTech client, M-DAQ, where he was General Counsel for four years. It was during his time in-house that the idea of Lexagle dawned upon him.

During his first management meeting at M-DAQ, Gerald realized that every other functional group in the company, from Finance to HR to Operations, used some technological platform or tool to aid them with recording, tracking, and presenting their work. Some examples of these platforms include Jira, Bloomberg, and Xero. However, no such platform existed for the legal department. Instead, they were stuck using traditional methods such as paper documents and filing cabinets. That was when Gerald researched solutions offering digital contract management services. While some companies were offering such services, he realized they were either unintuitive or overly complex for what lawyers or legal departments required. That was the moment when Gerald, who experienced the pain points of managing contracts first-hand, saw the opportunity for Lexagle to enter the industry by offering a unique contract management platform that would solve every lawyer's and company's contracting needs.

Contract Lifecycle Management (CLM) Industry

The CLM software market reached a value of USD1.5 Billion globally in 2020,[2] with the potential to reach USD3 Billion by 2026 with a compound annual growth rate (CAGR) of 12% for the next five years (2021–2026). With COVID-19 pushing the need to pivot digitally and working in remote locations, there is an opportunity for Lexagle to advertise to potential users and increase buy-in from them. As users become increasingly aware of CLM's role in the new norm, there will be a significant increase in demand for the best CLM software provider. However, the pandemic also poses challenges, and one significant problem has been the company's ability to expand its team due to the travel bans.

There are currently three major competitors in the industry: DocuSign, Icertis Contract Management Software, and PandaDoc. Others like Linklaters and Lupl are much smaller in market share and user base (Figure 1).

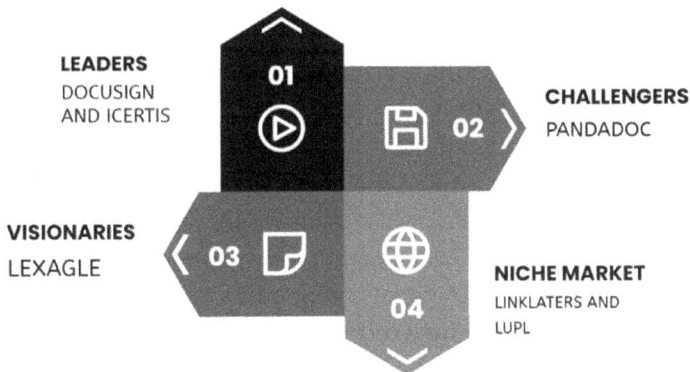

Figure 1: Contract Lifecycle Management competitors landscape

---

[2] IMARC Group, 2021. https://www.researchandmarkets.com/reports/5264072/contract-lifecycle-management-software-market

DocuSign (Leader)

DocuSign is the leading e-signature software whose primary product offering allows its users to sign their documents anywhere with any device. It has integrated with Google, namely in G-Suite, allowing users to complete their business transactions without logging out of their Google Drive and Gmail. Due to its high reliability, security, and performance, Google included the DocuSign app in their recommendation list for the G-suite.[3] DocuSign's customer make-up is as such: 40.3% of the customers come from small businesses (50 or fewer employees); 36.2% are the mid-market size of 51 to 1000 employees, and 23.5% are enterprises (more than 1,000 employees). One real-user survey shows that DocuSign is leading in user experience and satisfaction, as compared to PandaDoc and Icertis. In addition to all of the above, DocuSign offers free trials to their potential customers.[4] Demonstrating high market understanding, innovations, product functionality, and overall viability, Docusign is the industry leader with CLM revenues above SGD15 million.

Icertis Contract Management Software (Leader)

Icertis Contract Management Software offers several different products which fit into different categories, namely the SAP Store, Contract Management, Contract Analytics, and Contract Lifecycle Management (CLM). Unlike DocuSign, Icertis does not offer a free trial.[5] The majority of Icertis's users come from the enterprise (87.5%), mid-market (7.1%), and small business (5.4%) segments of the industry. It leads in terms of product offering roadmap and ease of doing business compared to DocuSign and PandaDoc.[6]

---

[3] About DocuSign, 2021. https://www.docusign.com/company

[4] Icertis Suite vs DocuSign vs PandaDoc, 2021. https://www.softwareadvice.com/contract-management/icertis-profile/vs/docusign/pandadoc/

[5] Contract Management Software Company — About Icertis. https://www.icertis.com/company/

[6] Compare PandaDoc, Icertis Contract Management Software, and DocuSign, 2021. https://www.g2.com/compare/pandadoc-vs-icertis-contract-management-software-vs-docusign

PandaDoc (Challenger)

PandaDoc offers extensive services which are categorized into different categories, such as Online Form Builder, Contract Management, CPQ (Configure, Price, Quote) Software, Proposal, Salesforce AppExchange, e-Signature, and Document Generation.[7] 77% of its users are small business owners, 19.6% are mid-market, and 3.4% are enterprises. PandaDoc is well-placed to succeed in the CLM market. It has a global presence and strong vision; however, it does not have leading-edge functionality unlike the market leaders. When compared against Icertis and DocuSign, PandaDoc leads in terms of ease of set-up, administration, and quality of customer service.[8]

Linklaters > Nakhoda (Niche market)

Linklaters > Nakhoda was created by a team of product managers, designers, and developers who worked together with lawyers and clients to co-create a technological breakthrough in the legal world (Linklaters > Nakhoda | Linklaters, 2021). What sets Linklaters > Nakhoda apart is its CreateiQ which assists in digital contract automation and the legal platform. In addition, Linklaters > Nakhoda also created the ISDA Create, which automates Initial Margin (IM) negotiations in financial institutions.

Lupl (Niche market)

Lupl is a legal startup company funded through collaboration between three international law firms — CMS, Cooley, and Rajah & Tann Asia. Lupl has signed an MOU with Singapore's Ministry of Law, leveraging its platform in assisting the digitalization of Singapore's legal sector.[9] Even while it was still in development, 500 firms from more than 50 countries were already on its beta waiting

---

[7] PandaDoc Mission, Values, and Team — PandaDoc, 2021 https://www.pandadoc.com/about/

[8] Icertis Suite vs DocuSign vs PandaDoc, 2021. https://www.softwareadvice.com/contract-management/icertis-profile/vs/docusign/pandadoc/

[9] Lupl — About. https://www.lupl.com/about

list. What sets Lupl apart from its competitors lies in its goal of bringing the community of legal departments and law firms together. With this end goal in mind, it is not surprising that Lupl is specifically designed for law firms, and thus all product improvement inputs come from users in legal departments and law firms around the world. It also uses an open API which allows collaborative work in a single platform.

Soaring Above

Derived from the Latin word *Lex,* meaning 'the law,' Lexagle is better known as the legal eagle. Lexagle offers the first AI-driven contract management platform to manage and coordinate a contract's lifecycle. With a mission statement that is "...*dedicated to building a platform that simplifies the contract process*",[10] Lexagle seeks to address two key value propositions:

> "*I want to better manage the agreements so that I can protect the company.*"
> — Communicating as legal counsel

> "*I want better visibility of my contracts so that I can manage relationships and close deals faster.*"
> — Representing a sales manager (Jimmy Tan, 2021)

Lexagle is a one-stop solution for legal contract lifecycle management, with the various stages of a contract's lifecycle translated into features within the platform. Lexagle rises above its competitors by emphasizing on User Experience (UX) to create stickiness with its users. Its dashboards and workspaces are aesthetically pleasing yet functional. Lexagle also provides different user experiences and interfaces for different types of users, from business and legal users to senior management. This differentiation is a unique approach to software design since most software treats all its users in the same way for efficiency reasons. Lexagle deviates from this tried and tested formula because it acknowledges that a contract

---

[10] Lexagle — Manifesto, 2021. https://www.lexagle.com/manifesto

involves multiple stakeholders in a company, each with differing requirements. From the in-house counsel trying to track policy compliance and consistency with past contracts to the business teams who want to get a quicker "yes" and, finally, senior management who wants a better overview of their contracting ecosystem. Lexagle provides a differing user experience to ensure that the individual requirements from the various stakeholders are properly addressed rather than to offer a one-size-fits-all model. Improving human productivity, driving user adoption, and lowering technical barriers for users are critical considerations in the platform's design.

Lexagle also rises above its competitors by being the first AI-driven CLM platform, covering a contract's lifecycle from creation (i.e., templates) to reviewing/auditing, storing, and signing. The platform replaces multiple competing products as a single platform, making contracts management more convenient and accessible. The AI-enabled platform uses natural language processing (NLP) and AI algorithms to perform contract summarization through keyword scanning but not advise on legal matters. Lexagle's AI features set it apart from its competitors. It provides data analytics, describes all ongoing contracts, and presents a transparent overview within the CEO view module (Figure 2).

One other unique advantage of Lexagle is that, as a Singapore company with a primarily Singapore-based team, the team can leverage Singapore's reputation as a politically neutral country with an established rule of law.

A Closer Look at Lexagle

Lexagle's platform manages the lifecycle of a contract through the key features shown in Figure 2. With user experience being the key driving factor when designing and building their platform, Lexagle allows different external and internal stakeholders to collaborate, inform, track, and manage contracts through an all-in-one integrated platform. Focusing on high user experience and usability, each of the features listed in Figure 2 is built with this key design

Manage all stages of the contract lifecycle with Lexagle

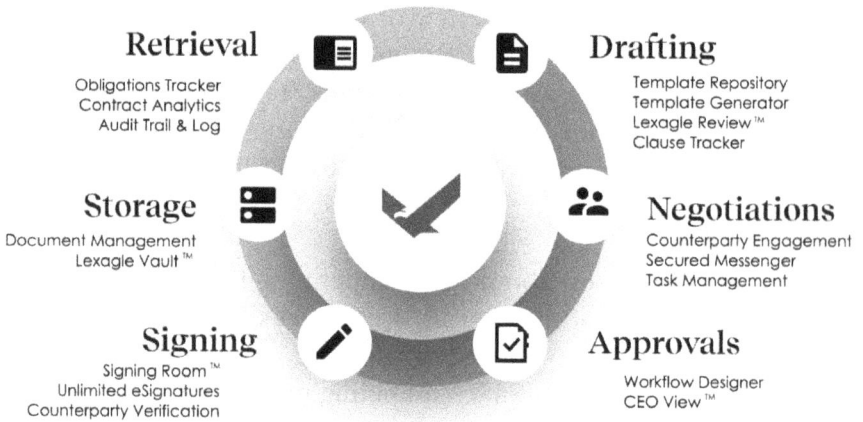

Retrieval
Obligations Tracker
Contract Analytics
Audit Trail & Log

Drafting
Template Repository
Template Generator
Lexagle Review ™
Clause Tracker

Storage
Document Management
Lexagle Vault ™

Negotiations
Counterparty Engagement
Secured Messenger
Task Management

Signing
Signing Room ™
Unlimited eSignatures
Counterparty Verification

Approvals
Workflow Designer
CEO View ™

Figure 2: Key product features of lexagle's contract life cycle (Lexagle, 2021)

motto in mind. These features become key attractions for customers who had not previously used any contract lifecycle management software, thus presenting a shorter learning curve, and reducing resistance to integration or adoption.

Lexagle's core features provide an end-to-end service for its users, with contract templates, digital signatures, scheduling, and notifications. Users can create contracts through the platform with its inbuilt contract template library and have clear access to all ongoing contracts within the company. Lexagle's AI-enabled contract summarization makes it easier for users to understand what each contract is about, helping them save precious time. Furthermore, Lexagle can remind users of upcoming legal obligations with its scheduling and notifications functions.

Lexagle has created a platform that is easy to integrate into customers' existing legacy systems, making it easier to onboard new customers and collaborate with them. The company also has an enterprise option for customers, giving them the ability to add customized features per their requests and helping to personalize the platform to meet their specific needs. The platform also has an inbuilt chat feature that allows users to communicate easily with all relevant parties, allowing for smoother contract management.

Challenges

With a value proposition that taps on a very traditional and unique problem, Lexagle has overcome many challenges in convincing its users to go digital. These challenges include convincing users of the return on investment (ROI) and security issues involved when using the platform. To convince potential customers of the ROI Lexagle could generate, the company had to first zero in on the problems of the existing legacy systems, and the negative consequences that their platform could help them avoid.

Legal documents and contracts have always had a high level of importance and privacy, which means Lexagle has to ensure that a certain level of confidentiality and security are available for its customers. Lexagle has an approval system that allows users to control who has access to view, edit, or sign the contracts to tackle this issue. Lexagle uses the cloud to back up its data in five remote locations for storage security, ensuring that customers do not lose any important documents that might arise from any adverse technical issues. Customers can also choose the location to store their data backups. Data and information security is such an essential element in Lexagle's solution that they have achieved an ISO 27001 certification, an internationally recognized quality specification for Information Security Management Systems.

The team

Lexagle's founding team comprises of Gerald Heng, Jimmy Tan, and Fayanne King. Having worked as a corporate lawyer, Gerald brings to the table what many of Lexagle's competitors lack — domain expertise. This has allowed Lexagle to better understand the pain points that lawyers and legal departments in the industry are facing, and is hence equipped to tackle them head-on with their expertise.

Gerald brings product knowledge, which has helped Lexagle create one-of-a-kind services. Fayanne, on the other hand, is the Chief Technology Officer who has helped the team translate its ideas and knowledge into a functional digital product. Lastly, Jimmy, who comes from a finance background, brings the skills and knowledge necessary to run the start-up and raise funds for the company. At the same time, Jimmy is responsible for the recruitment and Human Resource work required for bringing onboard the right talent for Lexagle's journey.

Together, the founding team brings different skill sets that complement each other. With a strong ambition and desire to move forward, they are continuously learning to improve Lexagle and what it has to offer. Besides the co-founders, Lexagle's team includes software developers, practitioners, AI developers, product owners, and business analysts.

Revenue & Cost Model

Revenue drivers

Lexagle's business model is subscription-based with two tiers: Freemium and Enterprise.

- The Freemium model allows non-subscribers to open, review, edit, sign, and store contracts. It is limited to these functions.
- The Enterprise model has all of the basic functionalities of the Freemium model, plus advanced functionalities such as CEO View™, Vault™, and administration tools. Enterprise clients also have access to integrations and configuration, e.g., branding, Single-Sign-On (SSO).

As all users can experience the basic function for free, no revenue is generated from the freemium subscription model. The enterprise model is, therefore, Lexagle's primary revenue driver.

Customers under the enterprise model are charged on a subscription basis, priced according to the number of users the customer intends to grant access to the platform.

Cost drivers

The bulk of Lexagle's operating costs are incurred by salary payments to employees, with the founders dividing their time and workload for development by 60:40 (Gerald 60%, Jimmy 40%). Lexagle faces no additional selling costs as the founders are the sales team; hence, the direct customer acquisition cost (CAC) is zero.

Impact of COVID-19

The COVID-19 pandemic has impacted Lexagle in two different ways: Customer Acquisition and Business Operations. COVID-19 has aided Lexagle in acquiring more customers. There has been a growing recognition that working conditions and practices may not fully return to how they were pre-pandemic, and this has sparked a growth in the value of digital solutions. As a result, on several occasions, customers even approached Lexagle for its digital solutions after simply hearing about them. Hence, it is clear that the pandemic has aided Lexagle in helping customers recognize the need to digitize their business processes by adopting their services. As the pandemic dragged along, more and more local and overseas customers have become accustomed to working digitally. Correspondingly, Lexagle also experienced significant business growth during this period.

COVID-19 has not had the same positive impact on its business operations. As a startup, teamwork, camaraderie, and communication are highly important, and the pandemic has made these aspects harder to achieve. As all employees have been working from home since March of 2020, it was initially challenging to develop a working arrangement that satisfies everyone. While that has since been solved, it remains challenging to communicate the Lexagle culture and ethos throughout the company as some may not have seen their colleagues in real life. The pandemic has also made it difficult for

Lexagle to hire new employees; hiring tech employees has always been a challenge, and these uncertain times have only worsened the situation.

Moving Forward

Lexagle's primary goal moving forward is to grow sales revenue for its current operation in Singapore. The company has recognized the growth in demand for its services in Australia, Indonesia, and Malaysia. The team is anxiously awaiting the re-opening of travel corridors to these countries to explore the feasibility of expanding their physical operations overseas. Furthermore, many of the organizations in these countries have chosen to headquarter their business in Singapore. These moves make Lexagle highly attractive for these organizations as it aids them in running their operations smoothly while being out of the country. Through Lexagle, these organizations will be able to negotiate, sign, and monitor their contracts from Singapore without the need to travel back and forth to make business decisions.

Chapter 3

RushOwl (A Route for Everyone)

Introduction

Singapore, in recent years, has seen rapid developments to urbanize land outside of its city center. With more Built-To-Order (BTO) government apartments set up in these areas, young adults who live in these newly developed, inaccessible regions now require a solution to commute to work directly and seamlessly.

Having identified these problems as both a uniquely Singaporean problem and a global problem, RushOwl set out to solve connectivity issues by creating their own transportation networks via a digital platform that connects passengers directly to fleet owners, smart city programs, and government organizations. Land transport vehicles in the RushOwl platform are on-demand, shared, and dynamically routed using the firm's intelligent algorithm that matches passengers' schedules and pools them together. RushOwl's team culture emphasizes on taking a data-driven approach to managing their decision-making process. The company is backed by Enterprise Singapore and Singapore Management University's Institute of Innovation and Entrepreneurship, which have played a significant role in helping RushOwl become what it is today.

The full suite of services that RushOwl provides to its clients include: Service Design and Planning, Technology Deployment, Launch Support, Data Analysis and Monitoring, Operational Training, and Performance Optimization. Its transport technologies span various use cases, including on-demand vehicle deployment from region to region, first-mile-last-mile (FMLM) deployment of vehicular assets, corporate employee transportation, midnight transportation, and dynamic-routing and smart allocation services for delivery services.

The Founder

Shin Ng, the founder of the RushOwl, graduated from SMU in 2020 and is a young graduate with a passion for entrepreneurship. RushOwl is, in fact, Shin's second attempt at entrepreneurship. Before founding RushOwl, he had set up his own business in 3D printing, churning out 600,000 fidget spinners in just two years. During his final semester at SMU, Shin took a class in Entrepreneurial Finance which he found to be the class he found most enjoyable. In the class, Shin worked on a project involving Night Buses. Through the project's analysis of existing business models and financial performance, he recognized the potential of this business. This was his first glimpse of the idea behind RushOwl.

A year before graduation, Shin made a trip to Hong Kong and was impressed by the city's public light buses transport system, the "minibus." Building on his idea for RushOwl, Shin thought of introducing on-demand bus services in Singapore that can carry fewer passengers while operating on ad-hoc routes with no set stops.

"Just click on the app, select a location, and the shuttle bus will arrive at the designated location to take passengers to their destination." This one simple line was how Shin introduced the RushOwl App. To quote a RushOwl user, "In the COVID-19 pandemic, our work timings have been staggered, and RushOwl was able to help me get to work seamlessly and directly to avoid human traffic."; they also said, "In the past, bus services had a fixed timing, so we often had to rush to take the bus." For office workers, who are RushOwl's target consumers, time is precious. With this in mind, RushOwl matches its users with shuttle services almost immediately, making booking and tracking these shuttles easily with the firm's RushTrail App.

Singapore's Transportation Industry

In 2017, Singapore's Land Transport Authority (LTA) called for tenders, seeking proposals from industry players for on-demand and dynamically routed public bus services during off-peak periods. GrabShuttle and Beeline were the first to answer, developing their on-demand bus services; however, both companies ended these services in 2019.

Beeline allowed commuters to book private bus rides using a mobile app, with its routes based on crowdsourced suggestions. In 2017, Beeline reported having 130 routes and 19,000 monthly bookings. "This decision will allow us to optimize our efforts and resources on developing products and services that can deliver benefits and convenience to more citizens," said Beeline, adding that it had "successfully served many Singaporean commuters" for four years. Since then, Beeline's code has been made open-source, allowing others to "take advantage of our codebase, building on it to create applications and platforms to help improve first-and-last mile connectivity in Singapore's transport system."

Separately, ride-hailing giant Grab ended its operations for both GrabShuttle and GrabShuttle Plus in January 2020. The two services differ in that GrabShuttle, which Beeline powered, operated on fixed routes and timings. Meanwhile, GrabShuttle Plus, powered by Canadian technology start-up RideCo, offered dynamic bookings similar to Grab's ride-hailing offerings. GrabShuttle Plus operates in areas such as Punggol, Sengkang, Bedok, Tampines, and Pasir Ris, as well as routes to and from Kranji Camp II and Sungei Gedong Camp in the west. In June 2019, these developments came after the LTA ended a six-month trial of on-demand bus services in the Joo Koon and Marina-Downtown areas, citing the "high technology costs" associated with offering such services.

"Services like GrabShuttle may not have been well-utilized and thus not financially viable for a private enterprise like Grab," said Singapore University of Social Sciences transport economist Walter Theseira. He added that operating a successful transit service is challenging to do so profitably, noting that it requires reliable demand and customers who are willing to pay. "On-demand services are (especially) hard because you need the demand to be just so. Too little demand, they're better off taking taxis. Too much demand, (there should just be) a regular bus service."

On-demand bus services exist in various cities worldwide, with varying degrees of success. Kutsuplus, which began operating in Helsinki in 2013, ended operations after two years as the authorities deemed it too costly. In January, Chariot, which operated in various US cities and was owned by carmaker Ford, announced it was closing shop.

Despite multiple case studies that failed globally, Shin remains very upbeat about the on-demand bus industry. "RushOwl has always positioned ourselves as a city connector instead of a mere technology solution. We believe that we are creating immense value when we take our technology not just to the cities that can afford them but rather to cities that will never have sufficient budget to create their own reliable, public transportation service. Singapore is where we start, but not where we will end." Shin mentions that his firm's direction is to be the public transportation infrastructure for developing cities globally.

A Route for Everyone

"RushOwl is public transportation for future mobility infrastructure for the people and unlocked by the people" — Shin Ng, CEO of RushOwl

RushOwl as a digitized mass transit network

On-Demand Shuttle Service:
- Dynamically Routed
- Multi-passenger
- Asset-light model
- Green / Environmentally Friendly

On-demand , home-to-work commutes at half the time of what public transportation offers, slight premium above public transportation service pricing.

Vision: "To provide cities around the world with better transportation connectivity."

Mission: "To work with all public passengers, businesses, and government bodies to enable smart transportation."

RushOwl can quickly develop and plan efficient transportation routes that private vehicles can take to bring users to their destination using data obtained from direct users. RushOwl's Artificial Intelligence (AI) algorithm also works with Business-to-Government (B2G) partners, such as government transportation agencies, helping them establish a public transportation infrastructure.

With many foreseeing the current staggered working arrangements as the "new normal," RushOwl is the ideal mode of commuting and potentially the future of on-demand transportation.

The AI Technology Behind RushOwl

RushOwl analyzes data from multiple transportation networks and uses complex algorithms to provide customized on-demand mobility solutions for its users. The platform can plan and route new details to improve the existing transportation infrastructure for government organizations and private transportation companies. RushOwl also uses the algorithm to optimize its fleet of freelance drivers for their commuter operations.

The unique dynamic routing technology developed by RushOwl improves transportation networks by assigning on-demand bus services to users, helping to bring them to their target destination quickly and efficiently. This feature directly addresses the concerns of long and crowded commutes in pockets around the existing public transportation network. RushOwl's ability to understand and translate existing data has helped the company develop a unique and valuable proposition for individual users and large organizations.

RushOwl is more than just an AI application. It is a complete platform that gives users the freedom to customize public transportation routes as and when needed, thus solving their own transportation needs in a crowdsourced manner.

A Closer Look at RushOwl

Target markets

A platform business model creates economic activities by connecting multiple customer types and facilitating successful transactions between them. Customers that provide products and services are known as producers, while those who consume them are known as consumers.

Governments and city authorities

RushOwl helps government organizations that are looking to develop their existing public bus systems, establish new infrastructure, or address any urgent rise in demand for transportation services. RushOwl's technology enables these service providers to meet the needs of the citizens with efficient and effective means of commuting. The community also benefits from the reduced number of on-road vehicles, smooth traffic, and a more enjoyable traveling experience within a more efficient transportation network. RushOwl's on-demand algorithm proved valuable during the COVID-19 pandemic, as government organizations needed additional transportation resources at a smaller scale to ferry people to and from quarantine facilities and hospitals.

Direct consumers

During periods of normalcy, RushOwl's consumer target groups are regular commuters and leisure riders. Commuters are groups of riders looking for an easy yet affordable transportation solution that will take them home or to work. This segment of customers is usually made up of recurring riders who have more predictable schedules and, hence, provide a dependable source of revenue to RushOwl.

On the other hand, leisure riders are occasional riders or tourists who want an accessible solution to getting to tourist hotspots, such as Pulau Ubin or Sentosa. The travel needs of these riders are less frequent and highly dependent on the prevailing travel climate; hence, they provide a less consistent source of revenue for RushOwl.

The team

RushOwl has two technical co-founders, eight software developers, and a business team of four, varying across sales and marketing departments.

Initially, Shin struggled to find people with the skill sets necessary to set up the revolutionary platform. However, Kris Lee, who was initially interviewing to be an app developer for the company, developed a strong alignment with RushOwl's vision and goals, and decided he did not want to simply work for RushOwl but wanted to be a part of the team. Kris is now a co-founder and the Chief Product Officer for the company. He brought in a junior, Song Yan Ho, who was involved in various future mobility trials when he was a student at the Nanyang Technological University, Singapore. Song Yan joined the team with his exceptional skills and knowledge and is now RushOwl's Chief Technology Officer.

Shin has emphasized on and appraised his team's soft skills, such as excellent management, motivation, and perseverance amid tough times. With many uncertainties and risks involved with running a start-up, these skills are essential in ensuring the company's success. RushOwl's relentless strive in these areas has helped the team overcome many obstacles and made the company what it is today.

Courage to Pivot

RushOwl was primarily a Business-to-Business (B2B) business that worked with bus companies as a Mobility-as-a-Service (MaaS) solution and earned via a monthly project fee and subscription model. However, the team found out that the B2B sector did not have progressive growth as expected. Therefore, RushOwl pivoted to cooperating with city authorities and developing for the potential Business-to-Consumer (B2C) market instead. The management now sees transportation companies as a resource partner instead of being dependent on them for business as Software-as-a-Solution (SaaS) adoption was relatively low. In February 2021, RushOwl's B2C revenue had increased by almost 20% of its total monthly revenue, and today it represents more than 95% of its primary business revenue.

Impact of COVID-19 on RushOwl

The COVID-19 pandemic has changed transportation needs and the way people commune. With staggered working hours, and rising concerns of being in crowded spaces (even on mass transit systems), people have begun looking for a solution to travel to their workplaces on time while minimizing interactions with other commuters and at an affordable price. The pandemic has showcased the importance of digitization, and RushOwl has captured this opportunity to present themselves as a company that can help these suppliers digitize their services. Between 2019 and 2020, RushOwl saw a 400% increase in its number of passengers, with most of them coming from connections with these newly onboarded suppliers. COVID-19 has helped RushOwl onboard many suppliers with this "wake-up call," increasing both the demand for RushOwl's services and the supply availability that RushOwl can tap on. RushOwl has been the ideal solution to tackling the many challenges COVID-19 has placed on the transportation industry. With its forward-looking mindset, RushOwl tailored a solution that is slated to become an integral part of the transportation industry moving forward.

Moving Forward

RushOwl is near completion of its test phase in Singapore and will begin pushing out full operations of its services soon to more developing cities. Some of these countries include the Philippines, Indonesia, and Vietnam. When asked about his firm's primary choice, Shin mentioned that Vietnam would be the first international expansion for RushOwl. "We believe that Vietnam is one

Our verticals

Geo-focused Advertisement Network

On-Demand and other digitalized bus deployments

Dynamic Routing Algorithm (AI-deployment)

Smart Dispatch Logistics Deployment

We're expanding to become a Smart City Transportation Network

Looking to work with:

Governmental Bodies
Countries like Vietnam, Philippines, Indonesia, Australia especially

Firms from Mobility Ecosystem
Partnerships to value-add our smart transportation network

City Developers
Cities who require our technology to leapfrog hefty infrastructure developments

of the fastest developing economies in Southeast Asia. Thus, we believe that our solution will scale quickly there because public transportation will be sorely absent among all the rapid urbanization and city developments."

Even with these clear objectives in mind, Shin's biggest concern is managing the company's growth. "I fear that a time will come where I cannot lead the company as well as those who have had greater experiences in managing multinational companies," shared Shin in an interview. However, Shin is fully committed to facing these challenges head-on and believes in the importance of continuous learning and adaptability. Despite these challenges, Shin has displayed his perseverance and charisma, having brought RushOwl to what it is today; he has shown that he has the capability of taking the company to new heights with his outstanding leadership.

Chapter 4

Trabble (Changing the Way We Travel)

Introduction

Around the world, the travel and hospitality industry has been known for its static and slow-to-change nature. With the COVID-19 pandemic, the industry faces tremendous pressure, and needs to adapt to new ways of operating and reducing customer contact with employees. This pandemic places Trabble in a position to leverage its technology to provide a solution that the industry desperately needs.

Trabble, launched in 2016, was initially a Business-to-Consumer (B2C) chat-based platform for tourists. However, by the end of 2018, the company pivoted to the Business-to-Business (B2B) market, developing its chat-based platform into an automated guest engagement solution for businesses operating in the travel and hospitality industry. The industry has begun preparations for the post-pandemic travel landscape through investments in such technology. Trabble's app is touted as an ideal travel platform for helping hotels and tourists adapt in uncertain times, creating a digital travel ecosystem that allows users to continue to enjoy traveling while remaining safe.

The Founders

Ian Low Jian Liang and Rys Bilinski co-founded Trabble in 2015. Ian began his entrepreneurship journey while serving his National

Service. Together with a group of friends, he started a gaming console rental website, renting out the popular Nintendo Wii for events or to those wanting to try out the console without purchasing it. Subsequently, Ian started his first company, Reactor, as a give-back initiative that provided educational programs for schools. Ian was able to bring the company to profitability within two years of operations before stepping away to pursue a career in his field of study — Finance.

Some years later, Ian spoke with a friend who was running one of Southeast Asia's largest budget accommodation chains. He rediscovered his passion for entrepreneurship and began thinking of a technological solution. He identified the growing popularity of ChatBots in the United States and wanted to replicate its success in Singapore. With the cogs set in motion, Ian began looking for a Chief Technology Officer to help develop the platform to bring his ideas to life. During this time, Ian met Rys, a UK expatriate working in Singapore. Rys identified with and related to the problems Trabble was facing and eagerly wanted to be a part of the team. With that, Trabble kicked off as a solution to help tourists travel better by integrating and working with local services to alleviate the uncertainties of being in a foreign country. Trabble initially started in the B2C market, but, through its partnerships with hotels, the co-founders realized that hotels and travel agencies were developing an interest in Trabble's platform. With the growing interest and strong relationships in the area, Trabble entered the B2B market, and the rest is history.

Hotel Industry

While Trabble operates within a very niche space, the demand for its services closely correlates to the hotel industry. The hundreds of thousands of hotel properties worldwide lead to a highly competitive environment where hotels differentiate themselves through price and unique experiential offerings for travelers. The future of the hotel industry will require some flexibility from hotels as they adjust to new trends, particularly from younger generations and business travelers who are looking for more leisure experiences built into their itinerary.

Global occupancy rates

The typical hotel occupancy rate is over 60% (Figure 1), with the highest rates reported across Asia and Europe. Occupancy rates in these regions range around 68% and 75%, respectively, in 2019. The travel and tourism industry accounts for approximately 10% of the global Gross Domestic Product (GDP) and is forecasted to grow in the coming years, especially after the COVID-19 pandemic once travel lanes reopen and border restrictions are eased. The industry's future is likely to be based on hotel fundamentals, such as convenience, internet availability, comfortable beds, good rooms, and excellent locations.

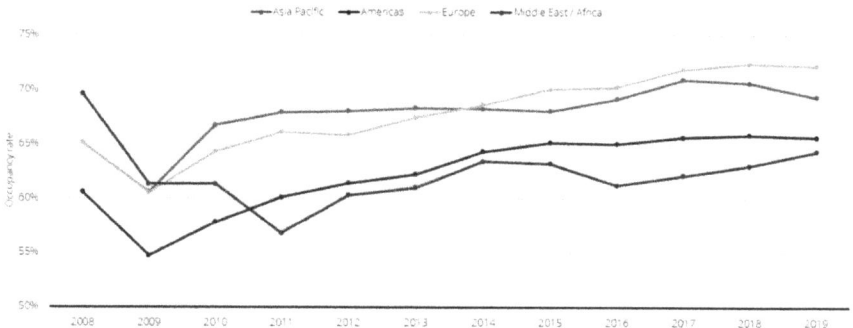

Figure 1: Occupancy rate of the worldwide hotel industry, 2008–2019, by region[1]

Competition

The rise of Airbnb could mark an end to the dominance of big hotel chains, bringing about disruptive changes to consumer behaviors. However, many countries have implemented regulations to curb the expansion of Airbnb, enabling big hotel chains to continue to assert their dominance over the industry. While Airbnb may be considered

---

[1] (Statista, 2020) *Hotel industry worldwide.* https://www.statista.com/topics/1102/hotels/

a significant player that offers the most rooms, it is best viewed as a marketplace for property owners than a hotel industry threat because they operate in very different segments.

Impact of technology

The hotel industry has not been spared from the demands of technology. Services such as Wi-Fi are fully expected to be present by modern customers. Such services are taxing to hotels, which already face competitive pricing, high commission charges from booking platforms, increasingly sophisticated apps, and more technology-related expenditures. As such, to support these services, cost-cutting has become of paramount importance to the hotel industry. This trend has resulted in consolidation within the industry, as evidenced by the vast Marriott-Starwood merger of 2016. The hotel industry has to deal with the increasingly high cost of real estate globally. Hotel chains will thus have to move to a franchising model to avoid the significant problems of acquiring suitable land for hotel space.

Typically, customers will view and explore options for hotels on their mobile devices, tablets, or laptops and proceed to purchase holidays through these devices rather than visit a travel agent for more information. Currently, 50% of total customers now book their hotels online.

Travelers are increasingly expecting a smoother and more personalized experience. They wish to be constantly connected, regardless of whether they are in a hotel or an airplane. Much pressure has been put on travel and tourism companies to improve their services and provide a better holiday experience, from booking to arriving at the hotel.

According to a survey conducted by Statista, 62% of respondents would like to check-in/out of a hotel via a hotel app (Figure 2), and 73% of them would use an app to open their door (Figure 3). The availability of an app would sway 47% of hotel guests to order room service (Figure 4).

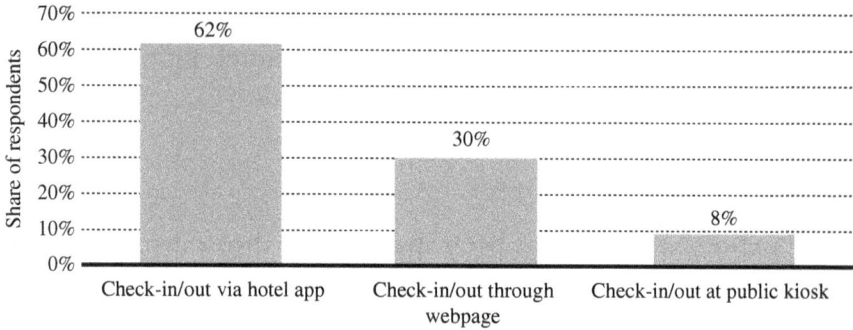

Figure 2: Global hotel check-in/out tech preferences, worldwide 2020[2]

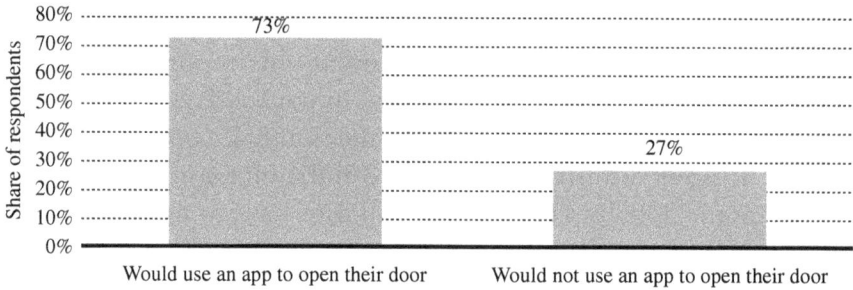

Figure 3: Share of hotel guests that would use an app to open the door of their hotel room worldwide as of August 2020[3]

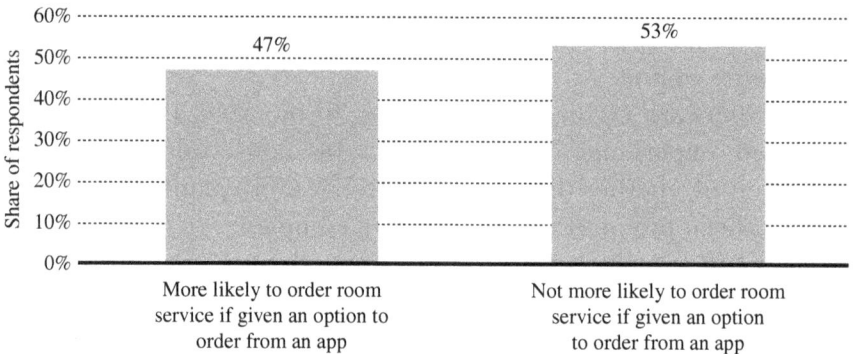

Figure 4: Share of hotel guests that would be more likely to order room service if they could order via an app worldwide as of August 2020[4]

---

[2] Statista, 2020 *Hotel industry worldwide.*

[3] Statista, 2020 *Hotel industry worldwide.*

[4] Statista, 2020 *Hotel industry worldwide.*

Changing the Way We Travel

"Consolidating the travel industry by empowering businesses to serve their travelers seamlessly through chats automated by AI" (Trabble, 2021) is Trabble's vision and mission. Trabble has created a Software-as-a-Service (SaaS) for smaller clients that have less than 100 rooms and at the same time an enterprise solution for clients with 100–500 rooms. These services allow Trabble to personalize and tailor its software to suit its customer's needs. With its services, Trabble aims to tackle two value propositions, which are:

1. Hotel Operators — "I want a common platform to achieve a seamless interaction with my guest"; and
2. Tourists — "I would like to reduce physical contact in light of post-COVID-19 conditions".

Trabble's in-app ChatBot guides users through reservations, inquiries, self-check-in, check-out, and concierge services, providing automated end-to-end solutions for hotels, travel agencies, and attractions (Figure 5). It increases operational efficiency, thereby reducing operating costs and improving guest satisfaction. ChatBot, an in-built

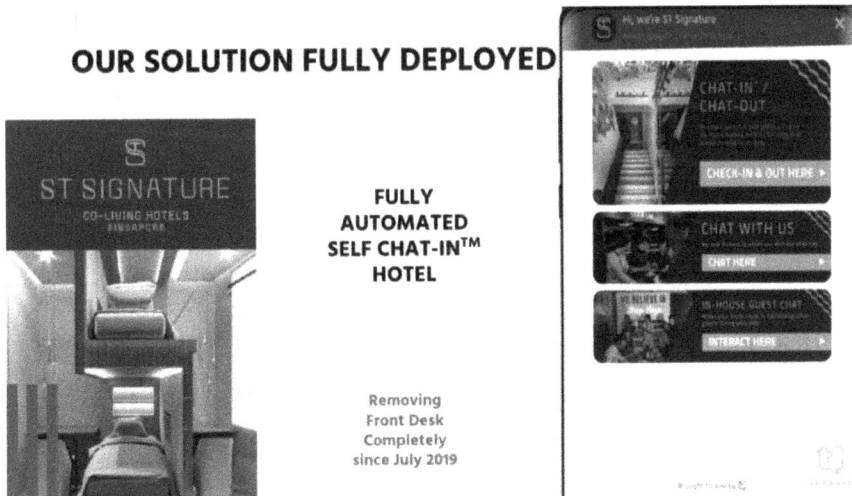

OUR SOLUTION FULLY DEPLOYED

S
ST SIGNATURE
CO-LIVING HOTELS
SINGAPORE

**FULLY
AUTOMATED
SELF CHAT-IN™
HOTEL**

Removing
Front Desk
Completely
since July 2019

Hi, we're ST Signature

CHAT-IN /
CHAT-OUT

CHECK-IN & OUT HERE ▶

CHAT WITH US

CHAT HERE ▶

IN-HOUSE GUEST CHAT

INTERACT HERE ▶

Figure 5: Trabble's solution

QUIC.KEY
SELF CHECK-IN SOLUTION

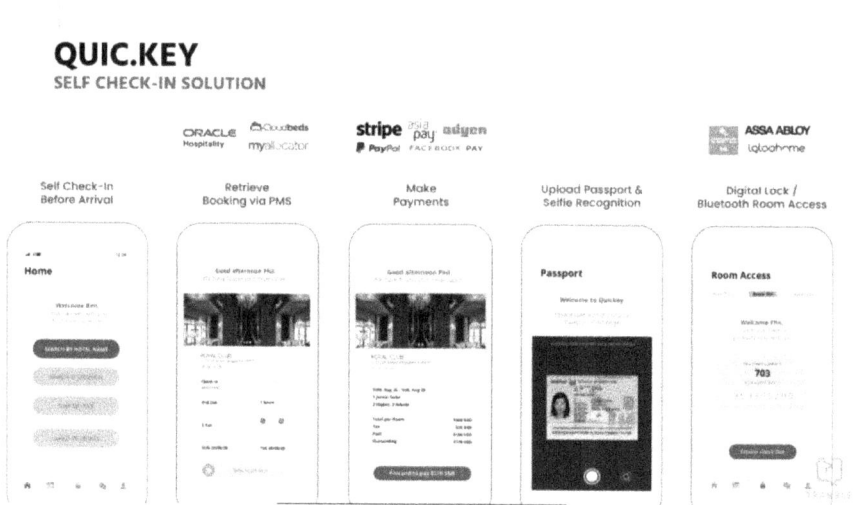

Figure 6:   Customer engagement service cycle in a hotel

chat service, serves as a platform for companies to communicate with their customers, helping them improve their customer service.

By integrating ChatBot with machine learning and Artificial Intelligence (AI), Trabble can provide businesses with the technology to better help travelers leverage local knowledge, resources, and services presented on their channels and in a format that best suits their customers. Along with Trabble's data analytics function, Trabble partners with hotels to analyze and identify customer purchasing patterns. The data obtained helps the platform to easily integrate with its customers' existing databases and is shared across its software ecosystems. This feature allows customers to collaborate and improve Trabble's software and intelligence, allowing Trabble to make smarter and quicker recommendations and suggestions.

Figure 6 provides an example of the customer engagement service cycle in a hotel and the role that Trabble plays in it.

Traveling from B2C to B2B

Trabble began its journey as a B2C platform for tourists who are looking to improve their travel experience but later re-pivoted to the B2B market. This change in the company's business model is a result of both push and pull factors. The major push factor that encouraged the company to transit to the B2B market was the high costs of incentivizing customers to use the platform, and the uncertainty and low frequency with which an individual travels. "Platforms like Grab, Lazada, or Shopee can give incentives to onboard customers, as the probability of them using the platform again is high. But, for Trabble, it is difficult to do the same as we cannot guarantee when customers will travel to Singapore again or how often they will travel overseas," mentioned Ian during a meeting. This uncertainty makes it difficult for Trabble to onboard B2C customers.

Fortunately, there was a pull factor, thanks to Trabble's strong partnerships with travel agencies and hotels, which showed a strong interest in the platform that Trabble was using to enhance the traveling experience. Trabble recognized industry players' need to reduce physical interactions and exchanges while maintaining quality services during the COVID-19 pandemic. Trabble was able to capture this opportunity and, through its SaaS, provided its customers with precisely what they badly needed. The strong relationship with its partners was a major contributing factor to helping the company successfully re-pivot from a B2C platform to a B2B SaaS.

What Changed

Transitioning from a travel platform to SaaS meant Trabble had to make alterations to its platform to meet the needs of its new customers (Figure 7). Many of Trabble's existing features have been repurposed and offered by their B2B customers, such as hotels, that have the same goal as Trabble of improving traveler experience, as services to their guests or customers. This outcome has helped Trabble with its consumer acquisition drive. It meant that Trabble no longer had to source for customers but rather could leverage on the hotels' guests for more business.

One significant change from the company's initial plan was the shift away from ChatBots. Initially, ChatBots were a crucial part of Trabble's operations, allowing them to communicate with travelers as the company did not have the resources available to attend to

TRABBLE'S SaaS

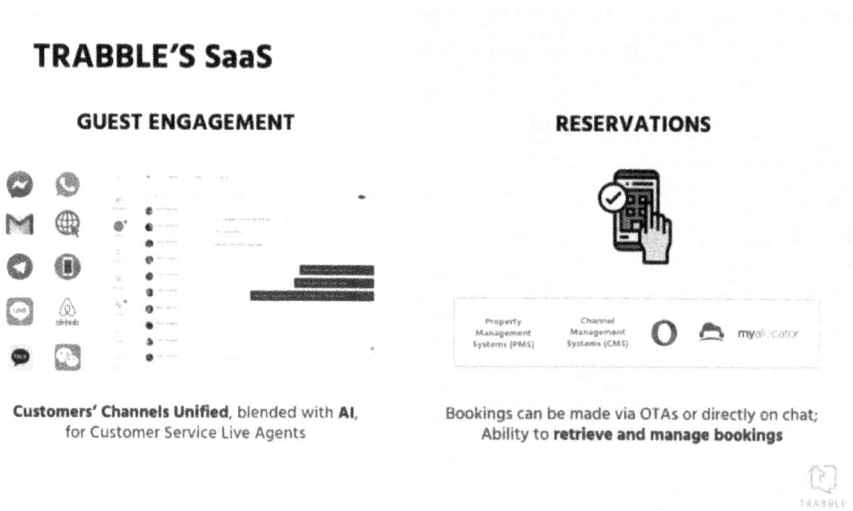

Figure 7:   Trabble's Software-as-a-Service (SaaS)

customer inquiries intimately. However, with hotels as their new target customers, Trabble could rely on their concierge and customer service resources to offer professional customer service with a human touch to users of the platform.

A Closer Look at Trabble

Target markets

Hotels, tourist attractions, and tour agencies play the role of producers on Trabble's platform. This group of merchants is responsible for bringing in travelers. Trabble can expand its customer base by tapping onto the guests and travelers who approach these customers for their services on the platform. At the same time, Trabble can enhance the services offered by these companies. As a platform that operates its customer service 24/7, Trabble can alleviate the need for service staff to be physically present at all times, thus allowing them to continue serving their customers through the platform. Customer service is improved as the staffing crew can serve users simultaneously and address their concerns more efficiently and effectively.

As an SaaS, Trabble's main customers in the consumer segment, apart from guests and travelers, are the staff of hotels, tourist attractions, and tour agencies. Trabble wants to help these companies improve labor efficiency by digitizing many of their existing services. These features would help them reduce the labor required to maintain high service quality and make more resources available for essential functions through redeployment.

Key partners

Payment gateways

Payment gateways such as Stripe, PayPal, Adyen, and AsiaPay allow Trabble to facilitate transactions, allowing users to make bookings and pay for other services directly through the platform. This partnership arrangement makes transactions more convenient for customers as they can link existing accounts to Trabble or key in their credit card details to make payments. At the same time, Trabble helps their partners increase their customer base; as Trabble's user base grows, so do their partners'.

Digital lock companies

By partnering with digital lock companies such as EQ Home, Trabble provides security for its users, especially when traveling in a foreign country. These partners are also sales channels for Trabble through their word-of-mouth recommendations.

Singapore Tourism Board (STB)

STB has authorized Trabble to onboard licensed tour guides onto their software/platform to serve travelers. This partnership allows Trabble to provide its customers with access to tour professionals, allowing them to work together to provide travelers with the best possible travel experience. At the same time, the partnership lets STB provide licensed tour guides with an additional revenue stream. With its credible reputation, STB facilitates Trabble's brand image and recognition within the Travel industry.

Revenue & Cost Model

Revenue drivers

Enterprise solution

Trabble uses a project-based model to implement its software for various customers to generate its main revenue stream. Each engagement with a client serves as a project for Trabble, in which the company charges an upfront fee for project implementation. Trabble then assesses the amount of effort needed for the developers to meet the specific requirements of the engagement. After estimating the project costs, Trabble charges the customer accordingly, depending on the project's complexity. The upfront implementation fees are meant to cover the work hours of the developers to customize and deploy the product while also providing a profit margin for the company. Trabble has stated that projects with minimal effort would amount to USD30,000 implementation costs for the client, while more complex projects can go up to USD200,000 in implementation costs.

Additionally, there is a monthly subscription fee for maintenance and support purposes. Clients may opt out of paying this fee if they do not wish to avail themselves of Trabble's service should they experience any problems with the system. The monthly subscription is 10% of the implementation fee for projects, travel agencies, and attractions.

Software-as-a-Service (SaaS) solution

Trabble is currently working on a self-managing and self-deploying feature aimed at smaller-sized customers. This feature would allow customers to set up their parameters on the platform without support from Trabble. By doing so, the customer would avoid the implementation fee charged by Trabble; however, the customer would still have to pay the monthly subscription fee to the company to use its SaaS platform. Trabble offers a range of subscription options at different prices based on the number of modules in each package. Any additional modules required by the customer will be offered *a la carte*.

Trabble also offers to sell the source code of the application to the client at an extra cost. This allows customers to make personalized changes to the application or hire a third-party developer to make the changes for them.

Guests can use the Trabble app to purchase services provided by hotels, travel agencies, and attractions. Trabble purchases these services at a discount by partnering with the establishments that supply them and re-sells these services on the Trabble platform. The company takes a 30% percent cut from customer purchases if they are made through their app.

Cost drivers

Trabble's team comprises 15 full-time employees stationed in Singapore, two developers in the Philippines, and one salesperson in Japan. This represents 90% of the costs of the company. Currently, rent expense is non-existent as Trabble does not have a physical office with online meetings conducted through platforms such as Zoom.

Impact of COVID-19

The recent COVID-19 pandemic has impacted the hotel industry severely, with a sharp drop in monthly hotel occupancy rates from 68% in the APAC region to 35% in May 2020, as illustrated in Figure 8.

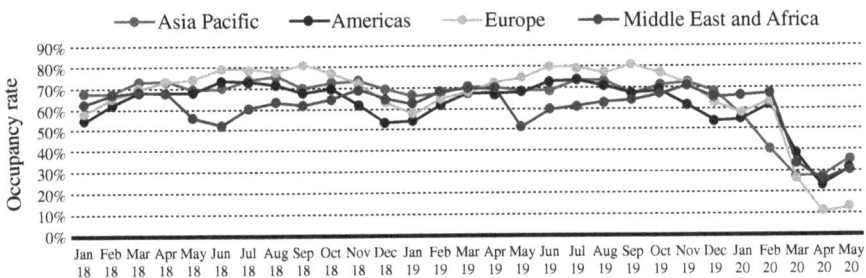

Figure 8: Monthly hotel occupancy rates worldwide 2018–2020, by region

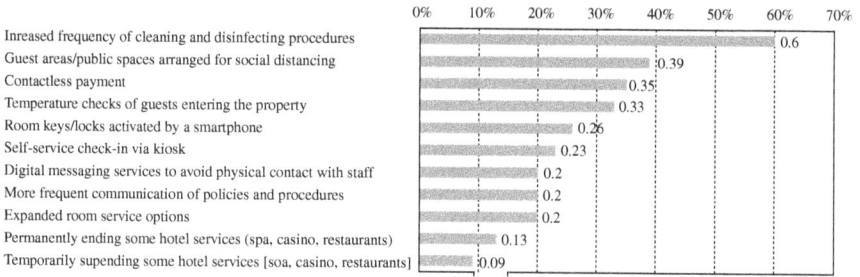

	0%	10%	20%	30%	40%	50%	60%	70%
Inreased frequency of cleaning and disinfecting procedures							0.6	
Guest areas/public spaces arranged for social distancing					0.39			
Contactless payment				0.35				
Temperature checks of guests entering the property				0.33				
Room keys/locks activated by a smartphone			0.26					
Self-service check-in via kiosk			0.23					
Digital messaging services to avoid physical contact with staff		0.2						
More frequent communication of policies and procedures		0.2						
Expanded room service options		0.2						
Permanently ending some hotel services (spa, casino, restaurants)	0.13							
Temporarily supending some hotel services [soa, casino, restaurants]	0.09							

Figure 9: COVID-19: public opinion on improving comfortability of hotel stays worldwide 2020[5]

The impact of COVID-19 has led to increased demand for automated hospitality services, with 35% of respondents wanting contactless payment options, 26% of respondents wanting room keys/locks to be activated by a smartphone, 23% of respondents preferring self-service check-in, and 20% of respondents wanting digital messaging services to avoid physical contact with staff (Figure 9).

The travel and hospitality industry was one of the few industries hardest hit by the COVID-19 pandemic, with countries going into lockdown and travel bans being put in place. Initially, this had a severe impact on companies like Trabble. B2B customers such as hotels were already difficult to persuade when it came to changing how they operate. With the uncertainty that the pandemic had caused, such customers were even harder to convince. However, near the end of 2020, as the pandemic persisted and business continued to decline for those customers, there was a switch in attitude as customers transitioned their view of Trabble from a "good to have" to a "need to have". These B2B customers recognize that, even if the pandemic situation improves, the travel industry may never go back to how it was before. The pandemic had accelerated the adoption of digitalized travel, with travelers wanting to check-in online, make payments online, and reduce physical interactions. Many

---

[5] Statista, 2020. https://www.statista.com/topics/1102/hotels/

aspects of operations that were not seen pre-COVID-19 have now become health and safety concerns. Trabble was able to leverage this opportunity, offering a way for its customers to continue providing high-quality customer service without the need for physical interaction. The pandemic has enhanced the value of Trabble's services as the way forward for the industry.

Moving Forward

Trabble is looking to offer its services in non-English-speaking developed markets with high disposable incomes. With the platform aiding largely English-speaking travelers, Trabble is considering offering its services to English-speaking travelers in a non-English speaking country like Japan or Korea. Furthermore, the cost of hiring English-speaking staff in those countries tends to be quite high. Trabble can thus offer a solution that reduces labor costs in those regions. Trabble is also looking to expand to less developed South-East Asia and Asian countries. As an SaaS, it is easy for them to deploy their services to these regions by selling the software to potential customers located there. Unlike developed countries, which may have the means to develop digital solutions to meet the needs of travelers, Trabble has identified a "blue ocean" in this space of less developed countries, allowing them to gain the first-mover advantage with their well-developed digital solution.

Trabble has begun communicating and partnering with Ali Group in China, which has helped them penetrate the market there. Trabble is in the process of being incorporated in Nanling and Guangxi, China. This partnership allows Trabble to introduce its technology and solution by collaborating with Ali Group's platforms and technology, which are actively used in over 400–600 hotels in China. While China's travel system has proven to be extremely efficient and effective when handling domestic travelers, the same has yet to be replicated for international travelers in China. Hence, by partnering with Ali Group, Trabble hopes to help them improve this promising sector of China's travel industry.

Chapter 5

Savour! (Savouring with Savour!)

Introduction

Singaporeans generated over 5.9 million tonnes of waste in 2020, with 665,000 tonnes or roughly 11% from food-related products.[1] Every day, tons of food are thrown out due to a mismatch between demand and supply. This wasteful outcome is the unfortunate result of poor communications between wholesale merchants and their Business-to-Business (B2B) customers. Katrina Lee, a fourth-year student in National University of Singapore (NUS), recognized these issues and decided that she wanted to develop a tech-enabled solution to help not only resolve these inefficiencies, but also tackle food wastage and insecurity.

Katrina co-founded Savour! in late 2019 to bridge the order sizes between what large suppliers offer and small buyers require. Savour! is a platform that lists near expiry, blemished, and surplus foods for the B2B Market.

> "Aims to empower SMEs, non-profits and social enterprises with savings via digitalization while tackling food wastage and food insecurity at the same time[2]."

---

[1] National Environment Agency, 2021. https://www.nea.gov.sg/our-services/waste-management/waste-statistics- and-overall-recycling

[2] Savour!: Overview, n.d. https://www.linkedin.com/company/savoursg/?original Subdomain=sg

The start-up struggled to find its footing during its early stages due to a lack of brand identity. Through perseverance and hard work, Savour! has more than 200 merchants to date and targets to onboard a total of 500 merchants by the end of 2021.

Savour! efficiently connects merchants and consumers via a digital solution that is accessible and convenient, saving time and cost for their procurement needs.

> "A one-stop cloud-based B2B e-procurement and sponsorship web and app platform connecting companies, non-profit organizations and school clubs to merchants to procure products and services at corporate discounts and in-kind sponsorship for events, programs, and regular operations in Singapore."

The Founders

Katrina Lee and Mike Sun are the co-founders of Savour!. Katrina started her entrepreneurship journey operating a Business-to-Consumer (B2C) e-commerce business selling fashion goods from overseas. Katrina Lee first experienced food insecurity issues in Singapore while volunteering with community service clubs and non-profit organizations. These non-profits, such as Willing Hearts, seek to distribute rations and food supplies to low-income house-holds and feed insecure families around the city. However, the recipients of these contributions occasionally turn down donations of common canned food and instant noodles as they already have enough low-quality staples and may not have sufficient space for the donated products. Katrina's experience in the food and beverage industry also exposed her to the considerable amount of food waste being discarded by restaurants and food stalls as they could not bear the costs of donating or reselling their excess food products. Disposing of them is hence a much cheaper and more convenient alternative.

Katrina and Mike first met during a Hackathon. During the competition, both Katrina and Mike pitched the same App idea to reduce food wastage. Upon meeting and discussing, they realized that each of them had the complementary skills they had been looking for: Katrina with the business know-how and charisma to onboard clients, and Mike with the technical skills required to create the platform. Together, they developed the idea of a tech-enabled solution that can better match the supply from food and beverage merchants to the demands of their customers, helping to tackle food insecurity and reducing food wastage overall.

Social Enterprise Industry

The social enterprise sector in Singapore is young and developing, with 63% of memberships in social enterprises such as the Singapore Centre for Social Enterprise, raiSE, being incorporated between 2014 to 2016, 21% between 2012 to 2014, and the rest before 2012. Social enterprises aim to achieve social outcomes in addition to being financially successful or sustainable. This sector is mainly dominated by early-stage social enterprises, with 19% still in their seed stage, 47% at the early stage, 28% in the growth stage, and only 6% at the maturity stage. With most social enterprises in their early to growth stage, similar to Savour!, competition is expected to be intense.

From Figure 1, it can be seen that the top three industries that social enterprises operate in are the Education, Training, and Health and Wellness industries, making them the most competitive industries to enter.

Savouring with Savour!

With a vision of "To tackle food wastage and food insecurity through their digital platform" and mission of "Empowering merchants with a social and environmental cause," Savour! offers a variety of benefits for both merchants and their B2B clients (Figure 2). Savour! aims to create value for its users by being a one-stop platform connecting wholesalers to B2B clients for sponsorships and corporate events to minimize the hassles of sourcing, communication, payment, and last-mile delivery. Through their platform, Savour!

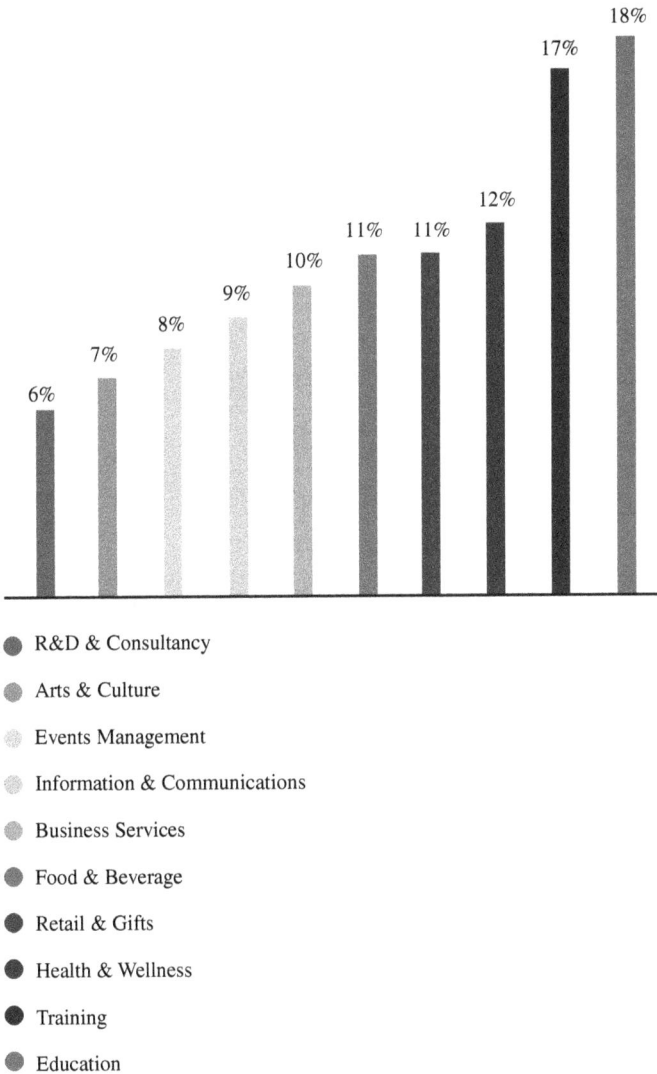

- R&D & Consultancy
- Arts & Culture
- Events Management
- Information & Communications
- Business Services
- Food & Beverage
- Retail & Gifts
- Health & Wellness
- Training
- Education

Figure 1:   Top 10 industries[1]

[1] raiSe, 2017 https://www.raise.sg/images/resources/pdf-files/raiSE—State-of-Social-Enterprise-in-Singapore-2017-Report.pdf

Figure 2: Savour!'s solution

serves as a centralized point of access with low listing costs, which saves significant time and money for their clients. With its expedient and transparent transfer of products, Savour!'s platform provides good product visibility and process transparency, leading to higher quality leads and solutions to alleviate surplus inventories.

What sets Savour! apart from its competitors is its provision of a one-stop platform for partnership managers, event planners, non-profits, and clubs to assist with procurement and sourcing sponsorships for corporate events and charities. Users of Savour! are given access to exclusive bulk deals with corporate discounts ranging from 10–90% off the retail price, helping them save even more (Figure 3). Besides food, Savour! offers their users the option to place orders for corporate gifts, supply materials, and event rental services at charity discount rates. From a societal point of view, Savour! aids the environment by reducing waste through reallocating expiring or blemished foods, and surplus products. Savour! is living up to its tagline of "Digital procurement to save you more while saving the earth and empowering those in need."

Additionally, the platform's hassle-free onboarding system for its merchants and B2B clients is easy to use and reduces the efforts for small and medium wholesalers to transition into the growing e-commerce space. Through the platform's inbuilt chat feature,

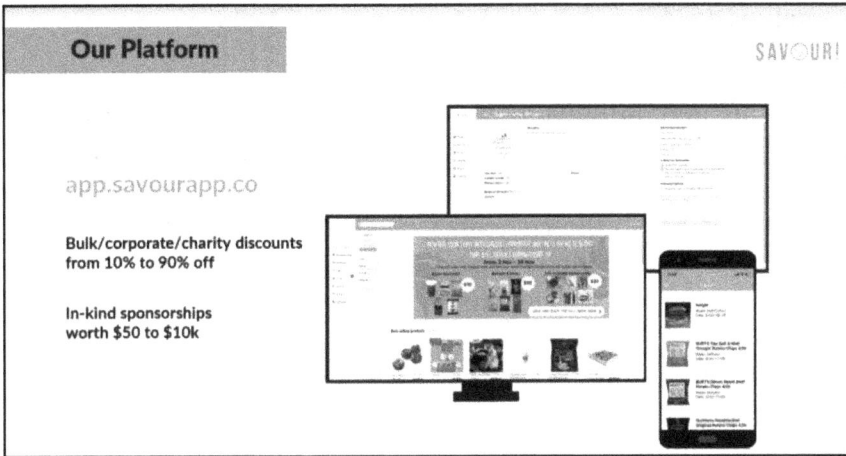

Figure 3: Savour!'s platform

similar to those found on Shopee and Lazada, merchants and their customers can directly communicate with one another. This feature has enabled Savour! to help merchants improve productivity by reducing wasteful communication and providing a direct communications channel with their clients. Overall, these features result in a highly accessible and attractive platform for merchants to collaborate with Savour!.

A Closer Look at Savour!

Thinking about the customers

As a cloud-based platform, Savour! is easily accessible from mobile devices and computers, allowing its users to access its services from anywhere, anytime. The platform personalizes customer experience by optimizing their online journey with the saving of preferences and order histories. The team regularly engages customers through marketing campaigns on various social media platforms and hosting webinars, live streams, and charity events. Users are also kept up-to-date with Savour!'s latest merchants, products, and discounts. As a platform business, Savour! connects two different customer types within transaction producers and consumers.

Target markets

Merchants play the role of producers on the Savour! platform. These include Multinational Corporations (MNCs), Small and Medium-Sized Enterprises (SMEs), and social enterprises that are manufacturers, wholesalers, and retailers across the supply chain. Savour! works with these clients to help sell their surplus products. Savour! can improve these organizations' brand awareness and serve a social cause by reducing food waste with its procurement and sponsorship service. Using Savour!'s digital platform as a new distribution channel, these producers can directly interact with other customers and grow within the network. As more B2B clients and merchants join the platform, Savour! can draw more buyers by increasing product diversity and sources. This outcome then leads to an increase in product awareness and transactions within the Savour! digital platform.

The consumers in the Savour! platform mainly includes MNCs, SMEs, non-profit organizations, and school clubs that procure products for regular operations, programs, and events. Through Savour!'s platform, these customers have access to exclusive deals for bulk purchases, charity, and corporate discounts. This feature helps promote the acquisition of excess produce, ultimately reducing the waste of perfectly fine products. Furthermore, the platform connects consumers with potential sponsors interested in supporting their causes while working together to tackle food insecurity.

The team

Katrina is the CEO of Savour! and is mainly in charge of developing marketing campaigns and engaging potential merchants and clients for partnership opportunities. This role is of high importance at Savour!'s current stage of development as it needs to increase its brand identity if it wishes to gain more traction with large organizations and charities in the future. Mike, on the other hand, is the Chief Technology Officer at Savour!. He is responsible for developing and maintaining the digital platform as well as implementing new features and ideas.

The rest of the team comprises mainly interns providing international perspectives and diverse skills, helping the company grow and develop. Savour! hopes to employ interns from local universities and overseas as the team strongly believes that interns are a good source of fresh ideas and perspectives that will help improve the company.

Revenue and Cost Model

Revenue drivers

The company's main source of revenue is earned in the form of commissions from both merchants and buyers. Table 1 displays the commissions charged to merchants and buyers for transactions on their platform.

As Savour! does not directly handle any logistical aspects of transactions made on the platform, its commissions are lower than those of other industry players such as RedMart (12% on groceries) and Lazada (11% on retail products). This lowered commission rate makes their platform more attractive for merchants to transact on and has helped them gain more traction with new merchants and buyers. Savour! has chosen to focus its efforts on increasing its revenues and commissions by achieving a higher transaction volume.

Cost drivers

The largest expense incurred by the company is on the development of its web application; however, this is a one-off cost. Savour!'s monthly maintenance costs are almost negligible and do not significantly impact the company's monthly financial performance. Most of the company's daily expenses are related to marketing and staff transportation costs. While these expenses can work out to be quite large, cumulatively, Savour!'s management believes (and rightly so)

Table 1: Commission rates

Merchants	Buyers
• 5% commission on expiring products • 10% commission on all other products	• 1% commission on sponsorships • 2.5% commission on other products

that they are necessary for growing its merchant base, gaining traction in the market, and developing its brand image.

Savour! does not foresee any significant forthcoming costs and, hence, is comfortable with its cash burn rate. The company is committed to attracting more quality interns with the right talents and skill sets necessary for adding value to the business.

Impact of COVID-19

COVID-19 has brought about many challenges as well as opportunities for Savour!. One group of consumers that was hit particularly hard are the food and beverage merchants. With Singapore's government imposing strict precautionary health measures, many merchants had to cease or limit their operations. At the same time, the demand for their services had drastically declined as more people had shifted to working from home. This led to an increase in the supply of surplus food from the merchants. Savour! was thus able to leverage this opportunity by providing a distribution channel for the merchants.

On the other hand, the pandemic had affected Savour!'s ability to host physical events which were earlier planned to help build its brand reputation and identity. This was a crucial step at Savour!'s early stage. Still, the company could adapt quickly and shift to virtual events, allowing it to remain competitive and avoid falling behind and losing out to competitors.

Moving Forward

As a full-time student, Katrina works with Savour! part-time, but plans to transition to a full-time CEO position upon her graduation in a year. Savour! is working on building and growing its presence in the niche sector that it operates in (see Figure 4). The team is also expanding its merchant partners through aggressive relationship building, networking, and marketing strategies. At the same time, Savour! is evaluating its sustainability and profitability of B2C expansion on its platform in addition to its growing B2B merchant base,

Timeline

Oct 21 - Oct 22
- Raise $1m Seed Round
- Increase horizontals
- Smarter product with better recommendation engine

Sep 20 - Sep 21
- Raising pre-seed funding of $100k
- Facilitate about $10k worth of transactions
- Boost partnerships and acquire MNC customers

Nov 22 - Nov 23
- Overseas expansion into overseas markets like SEA & Asia-Pacific

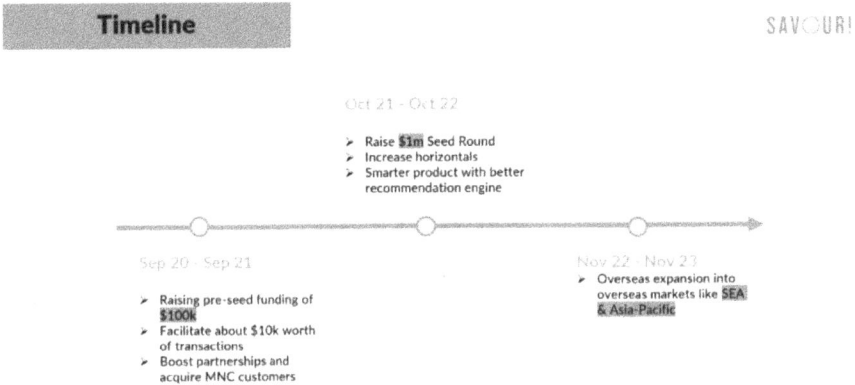

Figure 4: Savour!'s 2021 roadmap

and is working on expanding its offerings from near expiry, blemished, and surplus foods to include regular food, corporate gifts, and other office supplies. Savour! prefers partnering with SMEs who prioritize green initiatives and environmentally friendly values as a social enterprise.

Some of Savour!'s biggest challenges to moving forward are obtaining resources to effectively pitch their ideas to investors to raise funds and convince merchants to join their platform. Fortunately for Savour!, it has a low cash burn rate, no rent obligations, and negligible costs for maintenance of its cloud platform. This has allowed Savour! to focus most of its funds on marketing efforts to raise its brand awareness and improve its platform. This increases the attractiveness of their platform to merchants and makes it easier to get them on board. Some examples of what Savour! has done are in its marketing campaigns, webinars, live streaming sessions, and charity events to raise awareness of food wastage and insecurity. A number of its charity events have been highlighted on Savour!'s website and social media profiles, helping boost its brand image and showcasing the constructive social vision of the organization. Without the need for physical warehousing or inventory storage, Savour! has ample opportunity to scale tremendously through building its platform community.

Chapter 6

ThriftCity (A Smarter Way to Shop)

Introduction

Cross-border purchases are a daily affair for many in Singapore. However, faced with a rising number of products that are priced differently across different geographical regions, consumers find it challenging to locate the best quality products at the best price. Although online shopping has shortened the duration consumers spend on deliberating on which products to buy, where to buy, how much to buy, and when to buy, gaps in user experience remain within the consumers' journeys. These are the issues that ThriftCity has identified and wants to solve with its digital platform.

ThriftCity was borne out of a research project group known as Preferred.AI at the Singapore Management University (SMU). Professor Hady Wirawan Lauw and Darryl Ong led the team, focusing on entity identification and matching. The research group decided to transition into a start-up after realizing that consumers demand a tool to compare prices across e-commerce platforms. Using a combination of internet crawlers, Natural Language Processing (NLP), Human-in-the-Loop (HITL), and product matching algorithms, ThriftCity identifies similar products sold online and removes duplicates to present a clean list of aggregated search results for specific products. The technology requires high levels of expertise and is not easy to replicate but their technology can solve this problem. ThriftCity considers its options on two potential business models: (1) an E-commerce/Storefront model and (2) a Price Comparison Model.

The Founders

Hady Wirawan Lauw and Darryl Ong are the co-founders of ThriftCity. Darryl, a graduate of SMU, had previously worked with Hady, a Professor at SMU, as his teaching assistant. Having performed well together in the past, Darryl joined Hady on a research project which involved researching e-commerce data, looking at how user preferences were determined based on reviews and other product descriptions. They realized that much of the collected data was fragmented. It is common for users to spread their transactions across multiple websites, creating a significant challenge in understanding and developing a preference profile. The co-founders' initial motivation was to create a solution of "How to bring this data together?" from a research perspective. However, the team recognized that many sites were selling identical products at different prices due to varying pricing strategies. That was when the research team identified ThriftCity's value proposition of creating a way for users to find the best quality products at the most affordable prices across multiple sites most efficiently and effectively.

Despite having recently graduated, Darryl has a strong sense of ownership and motivation for the project. He has seen first-hand how far it has come and believes this is his best chance to be a founder. Similarly, Hady recognizes the potential of their solution and wants to capture the opportunity to commercialize ThriftCity. With that, the pair decided to embark on their journey of transforming ThriftCity from a research project to a fully functional start-up.

Industry

Storefront industry

Figure 1 shows some general market trends in the years ahead. Singapore's e-commerce market is expected to hit SGD3.7 billion in

MARKET TRENDS

81.5%
Use shopping apps every month

S$6.1 BILLION
Singapore e-commerce market size

7.7%
Growth forecast 2019 - 2023

S$2.91 BILLION
Cross-border shipping market in Singapore

73%
Have shopped from overseas merchants

Figure 1: Market trends

revenue in 2021, with a 9.93% (CAGR from 2021–2025) annual growth rate. According to a J.P. Morgan report in 2019, consumer electronics formed about 17.9% of the e-commerce market in Singapore (J.P. Morgan, 2019). This translates into SGD660 million in e-commerce market revenues for consumer electronics alone. The Singapore e-commerce market is dominated by three key players: Lazada, Shopee, and Amazon. The market leaders, Lazada and Shopee, have a strong backup from their parent companies and access to financial funding and other resources.

Using Porter's five forces analysis, the industry rivalry, threat of substitutes, bargaining power of buyers, and threat of new entrants are high, while the bargaining power of suppliers is low. Out of the five forces, four are unfavorable to new entrants. This indicates that this industry is highly competitive, consumers are price-sensitive, and it is challenging to establish oneself without sufficient financial resources. Given the stiff competition, any e-commerce platform needs to generate customer loyalty and entrench consumers to generate repeat sales.

Price comparison industry

ThriftCity's main competitors are Iprice, Priceme, and search engine companies like Google as a price comparison platform.

ThriftCity is confident that incumbents such as Google and Iprice would not develop the same capability. Currently, Google is primarily focused on web pages (online real estate) rather than products listed on the web.

The key drivers for the competition are the use of technology and data for consumer insights on pricing, user experience on the platform, logistics infrastructure (from order to delivery across borders), and search engine/mobile optimization. The analysis shows that industry rivalry and the threat of substitutes are high, the threat of new entrants is low, the bargaining power of suppliers is low, and the bargaining power of buyers is high.

A Smarter Way to Shop

In response to the problem ThriftCity had identified and prevailing industry factors, ThriftCity has developed a sophisticated search engine for online users to get the best deals from global online sellers. ThriftCity's vision and mission are "To provide purchasing solutions for customers" by "Providing cost-effectiveness from international retails and relevant product matching." ThriftCity uses a cutting-edge search engine powered by a suite of computing solutions, including Artificial Intelligence modules. ThriftCity uses crawlers, product matching algorithms, and HITL to parse and verify data online to minimize the listing of counterfeit products while enhancing the accuracy of the listings by removing duplicates and finding the exact products from a range of similar-looking ones. With this, ThriftCity can create value for its customers by answering the big question of where to buy the best quality products at the lowest available price. An example can be seen in Figure 2, where the prices of a single product across several e-commerce platforms are shown and compared.

ThriftCity has a clear idea of where its competitive advantage lies under both business models. As an e-commerce platform, ThriftCity can host suppliers on their platform or purchase goods on behalf of consumers, earning commissions in the process or gaining a spread from price arbitrage. ThriftCity can also provide price comparison

Figure 2: Price competitiveness

services for a fee. Compared to other e-commerce platforms, ThriftCity can simplify cross-border purchases while removing the complexity and risks of those transactions. Against price comparison sites, ThriftCity can better identify the best online deals as it can connect buyers with sellers from around the world.

ThriftCity is in a better position to help coordinate and facilitate transactions between buyers and sellers. With ThriftCity, users see the transparency of the costs involved from purchase to delivery and have a product warranty option.

A Closer Look at ThriftCity

Target markets

Product suppliers around the world play the role of producers in ThriftCity's platform. ThriftCity provides the suppliers with direct access to potential buyers globally to increase their customer base and sales. The company generates revenues either by selling its software to the suppliers or listing its products on ThriftCity's platform. The platform has automated translations and in-house currency conversions to solve common issues consumers encounter with overseas suppliers.

Consumers in ThriftCity's platform are online shoppers and people who use price checkers. ThriftCity directly tackles the pain points of such customers, providing them with an all-in-one platform to find the best products to purchase from direct suppliers. With the platform's ability to aggregate prices from websites of different languages, shoppers can find retailers who may not be listed on common price comparisons or e-commerce websites that offer better prices.

Enhancing the experience

ThriftCity has successfully brought the world to the consumer's fingertips, improving the convenience for its customers. As an online platform, ThriftCity provides access to various products globally through almost any smart device with internet connectivity. At the same time, ThriftCity plans to update its social media and instant messaging contacts with the latest deals, brands, and products on its platform. Thus, ThriftCity can engage its users to continue using its platform and increase the reach of suppliers on it. In addition, ThriftCity's algorithms have been able to provide product matching based on customer data, allowing them to make accurate recommendations and suggestions based on past purchases and searches.

Key partners

Online payment gateways

A standard service that e-commerce platforms require is online payment gateways to facilitate transactions. ThriftCity partners with online payment providers and integrates direct payment options into their platform. Many of ThriftCity's competitors lack this feature and instead usually direct consumers to third-party websites to make payments. The partnership with online payment providers affords ThriftCity a competitive advantage by allowing consumers to purchase products through their platform conveniently. At the same time, ThriftCity can help its partners grow their business and customer base as transactions on the platform increase.

E-Commerce platforms

ThriftCity plans to collaborate with e-commerce platforms using its price comparison feature and allow them to list products and services. Through this partnership, ThriftCity can increase the visibility and reach of their partners while saving on the logistics of running an e-commerce platform. Such a business model allows ThriftCity to scale and grow alongside the e-commerce platforms as their business expands.

Revenue & Cost Model

As ThriftCity has yet to begin operations, estimates were used for its revenue and cost models.

Storefront business model

ThriftCity makes use of technology to source the cheapest online seller for products. It acts as a proxy for the purchase and takes care of all the logistics involved, such as shipping, taxes, and even warranties. As users do not know the original price, the company generates revenue by taking a margin off the price differential and from the economies of scale achieved by aggregating shipping fees. It is well-known that e-commerce platforms, like Shopee, use internet crawlers against competitors like Lazada to offer price guarantees. Hence, ThriftCity can expect its competitors to do likewise. For long-term sustainability, ThriftCity needs to uphold its core competency (using technology and data to enable product matching algorithms) and offer other value propositions to have a substantial edge over its competition.

As Singapore's e-commerce market is projected to hit SGD3.7 billion in 2021,[1] the consumer electronics share of 17.9%[2] translates into an SGD660 million market a year. If ThriftCity can capture even 1% of this market, its annual revenue would be SGD6.6 million. ThriftCity recognizes that consumers will have concerns about cross-border warranties for purchasing consumer electronics from overseas retailers. Hence, ThriftCity also considers the costs incurred for the provision of a warranty for consumer electronics. The provision of a warranty would help ThriftCity boost sales and build its brand reputation. ThriftCity would need to keep its margins above the estimated warranty costs and always provide warranties to gain consumers' trust and confidence in their lower prices.

Once ThriftCity has established its brand name and reputation, it plans to expand its product offerings to include products with high repeat purchases. This includes possibly healthcare supplements and cosmetics, which are the third most purchased category of online items that comprises 7.5% of the annual e-commerce market. This translates into SGD277 million in revenues per year.[2] If ThriftCity could capture even 1% of the market, it would raise SGD2.77 million in revenues. However, it would also increase ThriftCity's business risk, as consumer electronics are more cyclical (consumers purchase less during the economic recession) than healthcare supplements and cosmetics (consumers still need to stay healthy and use cosmetics during an economic recession). Customers are meanwhile already familiar with the product details and available prices of B2C high repeat products.

Once its business has stabilized in Singapore, in the long term, ThriftCity can do a more detailed study and consider expanding its business to other Southeast Asian countries. This is to tap the wider Southeast Asian market as Singapore is, after all, a small marketplace.

---

[1] Statistica. https://www.statista.com/outlook/dmo/ecommerce/singapore

[2] 2019 J.P. MORGAN GLOBAL PAYMENT TRENDS, https://www.jpmorgan.com/europe/merchant-services/insights/reports/singapore

Price comparison model

As other price comparison platforms offer their services free of charge to consumers, charging consumers on a premium subscription model and gated information might not work, even if users can see where to buy 80–90% of products at the lowest price. Besides, consumers are already on the lookout for cheaper deals and, hence, being price-sensitive, are unlikely to pay to obtain lower prices. ThriftCity also offers its services to procurement companies and earns revenue per product search or weekly/monthly subscriptions. In summary, the monetization channel from the price comparison model is likely to be limited, and, even if successful, the amount could be relatively small.

Cost drivers

Under both revenue models, ThriftCity foresees staffing as its highest cost driver. As a start-up in the early stages of developing its digital platform, it is a crucial step in helping the company commercialize. ThriftCity is always looking to hire highly skilled software and AI engineers to transform their ideas into functional products. Another major cost driver is the computing resources required to set up and run the platform. However, over time, the company hopes to achieve economies of scale as software engineers can leverage the existing data to scale up the business and expand to multiple markets.

Impact of COVID-19

COVID-19 has played a major role in accelerating the adoption of digital services and the use of e-commerce platforms. As health concerns and restrictions are on the rise, consumers have turned to such platforms to meet their shopping needs. With the rising demand for such services, the pandemic has provided ThriftCity with an opportunity to penetrate the industry and launch its plat-

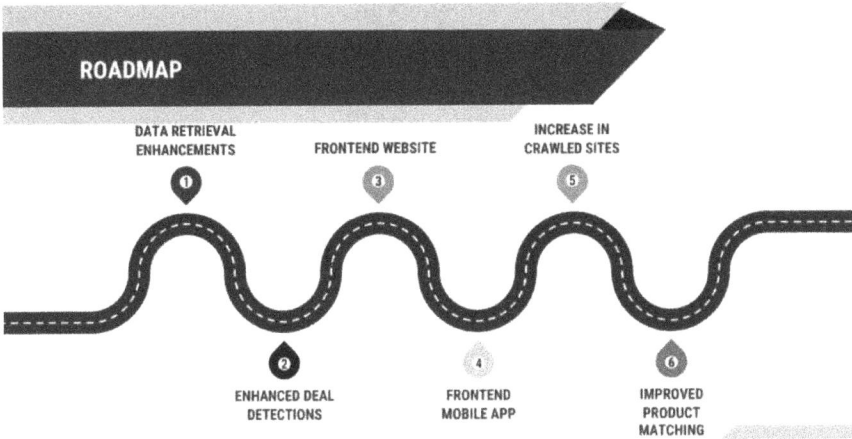

Figure 3: ThriftCity roadmap

form. However, as an early-stage start-up, the "runway" is short for ThriftCity to complete the development of its product, obtain customers, and launch its services. The opportunities that have arisen are not limited to ThriftCity, and the company can expect high competition in this space.

Moving Forward

Figure 3 displays a roadmap that shows how ThriftCity is transitioning from a research lab into a start-up to be launched in October/November 2021. The team has developed a website prototype, offering price comparison services. However, as ThriftCity is in the nascent stage, it is still considering options for an appropriate revenue and monetization model of either an e-commerce, storefront or price comparison service.

The company's primary objective is to pilot test its products with potential customers and validate the user market to identify which business model is most suitable. The biggest challenge moving forward is onboarding new clients. As a bootstrap, ThriftCity lacks the resources to convince new clients of their product's capabilities, making it difficult to showcase the value they can create for their clients. To overcome this, ThriftCity has developed multiple prototypes to help clients visualize how ThriftCity's platform model works and can benefit them. The company has reached out to several potential clients and is working to onboard them to try out the ThriftCity platform. This would provide them with actual feedback and use cases that ThriftCity could present to future clients.

Chapter 7

Friday.AI (Advancing One Friday at a Time)

Introduction

Singapore faces a severe labor shortage in professional healthcare. This shortage has increased the risk of overwork and burnout as well as affected healthcare providers' quality of service and care. The issue has exposed the shortcomings where many healthcare databases are not centralized and workflows are not interconnected. With healthcare playing an increasingly important role, especially during the COVID-19 pandemic, healthcare institutions must equip themselves with the right tools to improve their work processes. Friday.AI aims to empower and support healthcare institutions by implementing machine-learning technology and focusing on higher-order tasks and healthcare capabilities.

Friday.AI offers an enhanced digital platform targeted at private healthcare as a solution that matches professionals to customers' needs more effectively and efficiently. With many areas of the healthcare sector still operating manually, Friday.AI has managed to capture the vast opportunity to help digitalize the healthcare industry by alleviating the pain points of healthcare workers and improving the overall healthcare system.

The Founders

Elson Yong and Ethan Su are the co-founders of Friday.AI. The pair first met while pursuing postgraduate education at the University of Warwick in the United Kingdom. Elson was pursuing an Engineering Doctorate in Additive Manufacturing while Ethan was pursuing a Masters in Data Analytics. The young motivated team recognized they had strong compatibility and wanted to create something in the digital space to add value for its users.

The biggest motivation and trigger for the team to embark on their start-up journey was the COVID-19 pandemic. Both co-founders were very close to their grandparents and realized that the health-care sector was severely behind in terms of technological advancements. With Elson and Ethan's skills and knowledge, they set out to create a platform to revolutionize the healthcare sector to ensure patients and people like their grandparents could receive the best possible healthcare services. The company was initially called Famili, as the co-founders wanted to be more grounded to its consumers and represent something close to their hearts. Over time, Elson and Ethan decided they wanted the company to focus more on data analytics, particularly healthcare analytics. As an Artificial Intelligence (AI) company with a vision to empower healthcare professionals with the data analytical tools to help them with their work, the co-founders wanted a company name that more closely represented their vision. Friday.AI came into being because, according to Ethan, "Every week, Friday is the best day, and we hope that with the help of Friday.AI, every day will feel like a Friday, especially for healthcare workers."

Healthcare Industry

Hospitals/Long-term facilities

According to data from Singapore's Ministry of Health (MOH), the number of private healthcare institutions has increased slightly in the previous five years. MOH groups these institutions into six categories: hospitals, residential long-term care facilities, non-residential long-term care facilities, primary care facilities, dental clinics, and pharmacies. Friday.AI's target market includes private hospitals, private nursing homes, private general practitioner clinics, and private dental clinics. Friday.AI targets up to 80% of the market size from the total healthcare facilities in Singapore. It is projected that this will steadily increase by around 3.6% annually based on historical growth data. At the same time, there has been an increase in healthcare manpower (non-public) over the last five years. Friday.AI hopes to capture 29% of Singapore's total healthcare manpower market, which is projected to increase steadily at an annual rate of 3.5%.

Ageing population

The ageing population has been a recurring issue in Singapore. The government focuses its spending on improving its healthcare facilities by investing in technological advancements to enhance the current healthcare system. Technological upgrades on the various healthcare facilities and the introduction of new healthcare processes like teleconsultation will be the central focus of the healthcare budget allocation in the coming years. This is an opportunity for Friday.AI to enter the industry with its digital solutions.

Advancing One Friday at a Time

Friday.AI is an Internet of Things (IoT)-enabled infrastructure to empower users to make data-driven decisions, conduct analysis, and discover anomalies seamlessly. It aims to be at the forefront of the suite of healthcare technology that they offer, with the help of Artificial Intelligence.

Friday.AI serves as a digital healthcare solution using the Machine-Learning-as-a-Service (MLaaS) model that aims to revolutionize the current modality of operations. Machine learning technology can optimize and better manage the workload of healthcare professionals beyond current known practices.

Friday.AI creates value by increasing productivity and customer experience through automating processes and augmenting

VISION

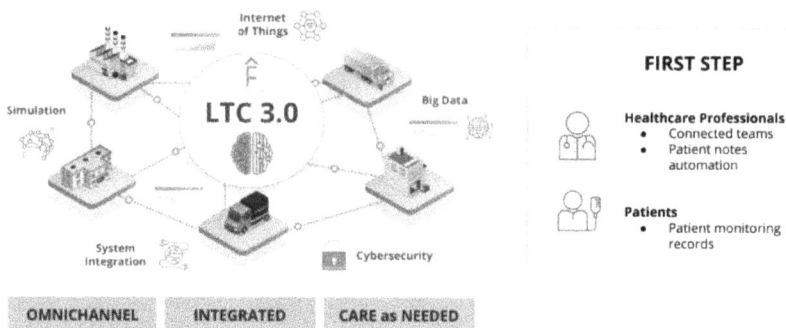

FRIDAY.AI

Internet of Things

LTC 3.0

Simulation

Big Data

System Integration

Cybersecurity

FIRST STEP

Healthcare Professionals
• Connected teams
• Patient notes automation

Patients
• Patient monitoring records

OMNICHANNEL INTEGRATED CARE as NEEDED

Figure 1: Friday.AI's vision

decision-making in healthcare (Figure 1). The company offers a user-friendly solution that helps healthcare institutions and medical service providers ensure their staff work more efficiently while saving costs. Friday.AI can achieve this by empowering data-driven decisions, conducting sophisticated analyses, scheduling and planning consultations, and identifying anomalies among patients seamlessly. As a local company offering IoT-enabled infrastructure, Friday.AI is a low-cost alternative that provides smart data-driven solutions through its machine learning tools, setting itself apart from its competitors.

The Core of Friday.AI

Friday.AI's customizable all-in-one platform removes wasteful processes in healthcare institutions with an in-built scheduling system, capturing data, unifying, and simplifying workflows. Users can access Friday.AI from anywhere with an internet connection, allowing them to easily check on patients, schedules, and tasks from the application. Unlike traditional off-the-shelf software, Friday.AI crowdsources data points from all its clients, anonymizes the data in compliance with the Personal Data Protection Act (PDPA), and extracts intelligence to improve the self-learning platform for all users.

Inventory order system & demand/supply forecasting

With its easy-to-use inventory order system and demand/supply forecasting, Friday.AI can notify users when and how much medication to order. This feature significantly reduces the administrative workload and allows healthcare workers to focus on the core areas of their jobs, which is to serve their patients. At the same time, accuracy and timeliness are enhanced by data-driven algorithms to reduce wastage and resource inefficiencies.

Patient management & schedule optimizer

Friday.AI's patient management system helps to automate workflows to improve patient satisfaction. The platform can automate demand-based work schedules for employees. This feature optimally matches employees' efforts to patients' needs, ensuring that employees are not overly stretched so that quality of service remains high. Through data analytics, Friday.AI can consistently inform users about their latest schedules, anomalies, orders, and other helpful information, helping them refine and improve their services.

The company has obtained grants and investments, which have allowed Friday.AI to create software at a low cost, making it highly attractive for its target market to adopt and collaborate to improve the overall healthcare system.

A Closer Look at Friday.AI

Private hospitals and nursing centers play the role of producers in Friday.AI's platform. They have limited funding and adopt few data infrastructure or digital tools. Friday.AI wants to provide a self-service and self-learning platform to improve inventory management and serve as a centralized hub for each department. Staff would then be able to save time and costs related to these administrative tasks. Friday.AI hopes to improve their customers' quality of service by simplifying work processes and better focusing their attention on serving their customers.

In terms of consumers on the platform, apart from the internal staff at private hospitals and nursing centers that benefit from the platform features, the ultimate beneficiaries are the patients, who can now enjoy accurate and timely services of high quality.

The team

Friday.AI's team includes its two co-founders, Elson and Ethan. Two other employees, Rachel and Michelle, are mainly responsible for developing the Friday.AI platform. Ethan has the technical skills and knowledge to transform their business idea into a digital solution. On the other hand, Elson has the soft skills required to help communicate their ideas to clients and manage the company. Rachel and Michelle are in charge of Finance, Business Development, Public Relations, and Marketing. The half-male-half-female team shares a unique team dynamic. Elson and Ethan are highly motivated and ambitious with their ideas and are constantly pushing the boundaries of how technology can help advance their business. On the other hand, Rachel and Michelle bring a pragmatic point of view to the team, helping to keep the business grounded while they validate and discuss the many ideas Ethan and Elson bring to the table. This team dynamic works very well as it allows them to constantly develop new ideas that are realistic.

Revenue & Cost Model

Revenue drivers

Friday.AI adopts a simple contract approach whereby customers are charged on a contract basis to implement Friday.AI's platform and infrastructure. The company also offers maintenance contracts that include systems updating. The cost of each contract depends on the size, scale, and duration of implementation.

Cost Drivers

The main cost drivers for the company are manpower costs. Other cost drivers include the technology aspects such as hardware acquisition and maintenance costs required to run the Friday.AI platform. As a start-up, marketing expenses are incurred to help build the brand's image and reputation.

Impact of COVID-19

COVID-19 has highlighted the importance of the healthcare industry and the need to ensure the safety and welfare of non-COVID-19 patients in hospitals. The pandemic has led organizations in this industry to recognize the need to digitize and improve their operations. COVID-19 has unearthed new issues for the industry in terms of staffing. In the past, it was easy to hire manpower from overseas. The pandemic has limited this capability as travel bans are put in place, and several countries are holding on to their healthcare providers. The pandemic has increased the willingness of industry players to adopt new digital solutions to resolve these challenging issues. Healthcare institutions can limit the exposure of non-COVID-19 patients in hospitals by using digital tools such as schedulers. With digitalization, healthcare staff can also maximize their time and efforts to attend to more patients without compromising the quality of healthcare that they provide.

Moving Forward

One of the midterm plans of Friday.AI is to branch out to private general practitioner clinics (GPs) as there is a big market potential given the sheer volume of these types of clinics (Figure 2). Introducing it to this segment would help in expanding their reach from larger institutions. Friday.AI could offer their digital solution at a lower price than other products in the market because of their subsidized grants and investments. The nature of GPs is such that they would be more inclined to avail themselves of the product if it is a cheaper alternative, especially if the product had been tried and tested by other healthcare institutions. This expansion is envisaged to take 3 to 5 years as Friday.AI is currently still trying to establish its footing in nursing homes and private hospitals.

MARKET SIZING ──────────────────────── FRIDAY.AI

Penetration of 20% of the market in Singapore

31 Private Nursing Homes

12,020 Direct Care Nurses

S$240 per nurse p.a*

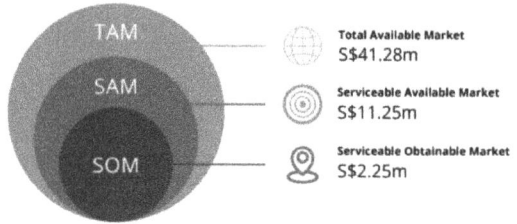

TAM — Total Available Market
S$41.28m

SAM — Serviceable Available Market
S$11.25m

SOM — Serviceable Obtainable Market
S$2.25m

Figure 2:   Friday.AI's market size

Friday.AI is looking to expand to other countries in Asia with an aging population like Japan, Korea, and Thailand in the longer term. However, a challenge that they need to address is the localization of the software, especially in the linguistic content of the service. Most of these countries operate in their native language, and Friday.AI needs to use the appropriate native language to enter the new markets.

Chapter 8

Kura Kura (The Lovable Kura)

Introduction

Singapore is home to over 37,400 international companies and is the headquarters of many companies within the Asia Pacific region. A significant global player in trade and finance, Singapore is also known to be a work-driven society. The working culture in Singapore is influenced by the need to maintain a competitive economy powered by high levels of productivity due to its small population. In 2019, Singapore ranked 32 among 40 countries with the worst work-life balance and ranked second highest for work intensity which factors in vacation time and working hours per week.[1] Based on a Singapore employee survey conducted by United Overseas Bank (UOB), 89% reported the need to work long hours throughout the week to ensure job security.[2]

In 2019, the World Health Organisation (WHO) officially recognized burn-out as an occupational element deserving attention to overall wellness in the workplace. Despite Singapore's economic success and developed social environment, employee stress contributes to deteriorating mental health, with burn-out almost inevitable in

---

[1] Straits Times, 2019 https://www.straitstimes.com/business/singapore-ranks-32-out-of-40-in-new-index-on-work-life-balance
[2] The Business Times, 2015 https://www.businesstimes.com.sg/government-economy/three-quarters-of-singapore-employees-expect-work-life-balance-to-improve-from

most adults' working lives. In addition, employee burn-outs can lead to long-term costs to employers in the form of increased annual healthcare spending, higher rates of sick leave, and lower productivity. Moreover, seeking help with matters associated with mental illness among Singaporeans may be viewed as a stigma.

Every day, occupational employees are subject to long working hours and demanding schedules. Along with the recent COVID-19 restrictions, more and more professionals struggle with increased stress-induced medical conditions amid limited ways of initiating self-care practices. These are just some of the issues Arif and Veric have set out to address with their start-up platform, Kura Kura.

Kura Kura is a Software-as-a-Service (SaaS) enterprise platform (app) for individuals in the workplace that provides a way to make mental wellness fun and accessible. Employees can effectively lower their stress and anxiety levels while playing games and interacting with their personalized digital pet (Kura).

The Founders

Co-founders Arif Woozeer and Veric Tan have been close friends since high school. At the peak of the COVID-19 pandemic, they witnessed the mental health struggles within their community first-hand. In their attempt to combat personal encounters with burn-out, they turned to mobile apps to find ways of managing stress and keeping positive while balancing their hectic schedules. They tried several apps but found it challenging to stay motivated to continue using them and quickly lost interest. Arif and Veric thought they could offer a product that would provide aspects of wellness while delivering fun and engagement mechanisms to users. Thus, they began ideating a different approach to wellness and spent many hours developing creative ideas. They launched semi-publicly during several hackathon events in the US and Singapore. In time, they began to realize that their idea had commercial value.

Mental Wellness Industry

Stress ascribed to COVID-19 has exacerbated the already rising stress levels due to intense work environments over the past several years, resulting in the increasingly popular health tracking apps. The upsurge of workloads paired with the cutback of work-life balance has harmed the global population's emotional, physical, and mental states. Health tracking applications have had a positive impact, providing beneficial outlets encompassing fitness, sleep, mindfulness, well-being, and nutrition. According to Verified Market Research, the global health and fitness app market was valued at USD3.45 billion in 2019, projected to reach USD15.6 billion by 2027, growing at a compound annual growth rate (CAGR) of 20.81% from 2020 to 2027.[3] Although health and wellness apps have captured some of this segment, fitness apps dominate the field. Statista reported approximately 47,140 health apps on the market in the Google play store.[4] Challenges faced by those entering this crowded space include software transferability and cost, data security and privacy, and network access and reliability. Some of Kura Kura's main competitors are Mindfi, Aura, Happiness Trainer, and Happify.

With numerous wellness apps available in the market, the industry demands high differentiation and brand development for entrants like Kura Kura to succeed. Many mindfulness apps provide similar services in the market, some of which are well-known and do not charge a fee. There are no proprietary restrictions in the mindfulness app space in Singapore, making it easy for entrants to create similar apps and enter the industry. New entrants will then have to focus on marketing and customer acquisition efforts to remain competitive. Kura Kura is thus entering and competing in a highly competitive market that has limited profitability due to its ease of entry and the presence of strong competitors with established reputations.

---

[3]Verified Market Research, 2021 https://www.verifiedmarketresearch.com/product/health-and-fitness-app-market/
[4]Statista, 2021 https://www.statista.com/statistics/779919/health-apps-available-google-play-worldwide/

The Lovable Kura

Kura Kura offers a unique value proposition of mental wellness by delivering a self-service platform for users who are ready to improve their mental health through narrative-driven games, reflections, and mental therapeutics. Kura Kura users start the healing process by adopting a loveable virtual turtle (named Kura) and building a relationship with this affable creature which has a symbiotic relationship with individual well-being. Their stated mission is "Making wellness second nature for a kinder world" (Figure 1).

Kura's well-being is directly tied to its owner's actions to improve their mental health. The more users take care of themselves through mindfulness and positive reinforcement, the more wholesome Kura will be. Through interactions with Kura that go through several stages of growth and development according to users' care and attention, users experience a journey with a friend that they care for and receive love in return. This shared journey is incredibly engaging for users to improve their mental health and grow together with Kura (Figure 2).

Figure 1:   Kura Kura's mission

grow with kura

complete reflections to level up!

Stage 1   **Stage 2**   **Stage 3**

Figure 2: Growing with Kura

Kura Kura, as a platform centered on mental wellness ownership, adopts curated solutions by professional psychologists. The
suite of tools on Kura Kura is not only for stress relief but also for
pivoting harmful strains of thoughts into positive self-reflection
through gaming and guided activities for each user.

Besides improving mental wellness, Kura Kura has a mission to
remove the stigma around mental illness and improve the way people approach and handle a previously taboo topic.

> "We do not see ourselves as a clinical solution to mental health, but
> we are a platform that will alleviate some of the consequences of
> living in a stressful society."
>
> — Arif Woozer, Co-Founder of Kura Kura

A Different Point-of-View

Although today's app landscape offers many choices, Kura Kura
stands out from its competition by providing a gamification model
through a virtual pet and reflection algorithm that promotes higher
engagement and retention rates. Unlike most of their competitors,
Kura Kura has managed to gain professional advice and solutions
from industrial psychologists. Many of the application's features are
co-developed with these experts.

Kura Kura also offers mentorship services and social groups through its platform for users to personalize their friendship circle and share experiences as part of the healing process. This feature lets users connect with friends or other users on the app, keeping track of how each other's Kura is doing with added communication and interactions. The platform creates a safe environment for the community to share their struggles and ask for help without feeling awkward.

Kura Kura provides a platform that encourages the community to collaborate. An example is the weekly challenges (Figure 3). Every week, users are given a challenge based on tenets of positive psychology and encouraged to report the outcomes of their weekly

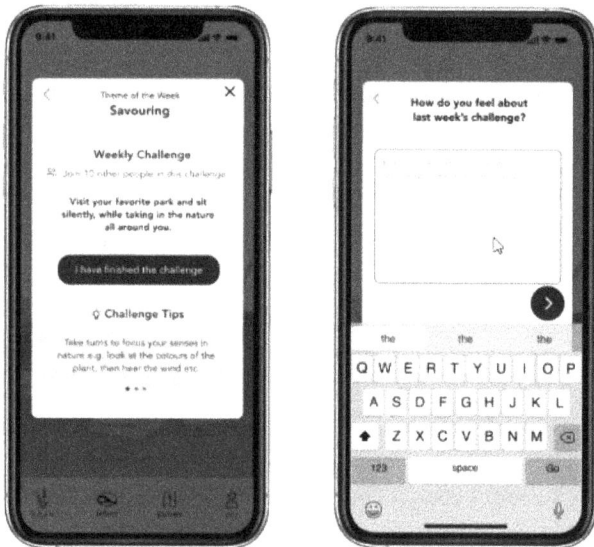

Weekly Challenge

Users are tasked with a weekly challenge based off the carefully curated list of wellness tenants.

Figure 3:   Weekly challenges

challenge to help their Kura grow. Users can view the number of participants in the challenge and post their inputs publicly for others to view. This feature allows users to read each other's input and share their positive experiences to accelerate healing.

A Closer Look at Kura Kura

Target market

Kura Kura's business consumers are the Human Resource (HR) departments of various organizations with employee wellness initiatives to engage and motivate employees for increased productivity and retention rates. In this mode, the Kura Kura application takes care of the organization's in-house mental wellness programs and directly interfaces with employees. Kura Kura's app-based platform allows employers to offer their employees a means to reconnect with themselves through mindfulness exercises and affirmation wickets. Employers can also gain better insights into where employees feel burned out or stressed and offer support using destressing and mindfulness techniques through Kura Kura.

Kura Kura's target market for retail consumers is the 18 to 34 year-old age group. Internal market research found this group to resonate the most with its app. Typically, young to middle-aged professionals within this age demographic work in demanding occupations that take a toll on their physical and mental health. Furthermore, this age group has a mindful culture that supports individual plights.

Kura Kura is also targeting younger children by appealing to parents concerned for their children's mental wellness. The competitive nature of Singapore's stellar education system is stressful to many children. Kura Kura's gaming-focused platform is a great fit for kids to take care of their mental health.

Interesting features

Besides the pet Kura, the app has exciting features for a personalized experience toward mental wellness, such as music reflection and the Ninja Pad game (Figure 4).

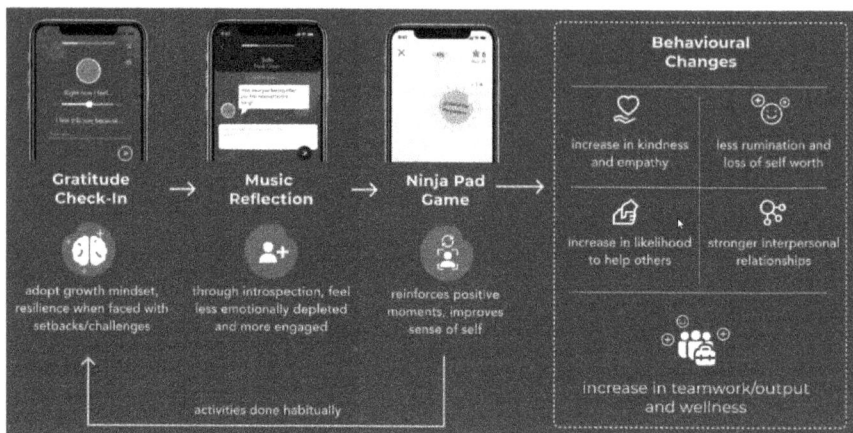

Figure 4:   Kura Kura's features

Music reflection

The music reflection feature allows users to choose their favorite songs that they want the app to play and engage them in a meaningful reflection session. Research has shown that people use music to relieve stress as a form of catharsis, and Kura Kura uses it to connect with their users' emotions. While the app plays the songs, the platform prompts the user with questions like "How does the music make you feel?" or "Do you have any memories associated with the song?" Users can better understand their feelings through this process, while Kura Kura continuously learns from the data points gathered from each interaction.

Ninja Pad Game

Kura Kura uses the Ninja Pad Game to encourage positive reinforcement. The game extracts users' emotions, reflections, and other data points in their Gratitude Check-in and Music Reflection to create lily pads within the interface. Users are then required to select the lily pads with positive emotions to progress through the game. This interaction encourages users to think positively about themselves and their environment.

Continuous improvements with data and guidance

Kura Kura's app uses multiple data points such as user frequency, Kura's health, Ecosystem interaction, "Stress-Buzzer" usage, user rating, and feedback loops to improve its model. Having completed an alpha release with 100 users, Kura Kura will be running active pilots in collaboration with Institutes of Higher Learning (IHLs) and non-profit organizations throughout Singapore.

Revenue & Cost Model

Revenue and cost drivers

Organizations will be able to garner feedback on the individual wellness of their employees and their work department. Most of the company's current revenues come from companies engaged in their pilot testing phases. Kura Kura is also working on a Freemium model for its Business-to-Consumer (B2C) users to get a feel of how the app works and experience the features it offers. Kura Kura's main cost drivers are those relating to staffing and running the application. Costs relating to maintaining the software are expected to be negligible once the company has commercialized the app.

Impact of COVID-19

Kura Kura is a product developed in light of the COVID-19 pandemic. During uncertain times, Singaporean society has faced increasing stress, and individuals and organizations are becoming more aware of the importance of managing mental wellness. As mental wellness has transformed from good-to-have to need-to-have, Kura Kura is well placed to enter the market with its solution. Furthermore, with the pandemic reducing physical operations and interactions, the adoption of digital solutions like Kura Kura becomes more appealing to potential customers and investors.

Moving Forward

Looking ahead, Kura Kura expects to onboard enterprise deals by the end of 2022 and hopes to consolidate its consumers and develop a pre-trained algorithm that can detect users' mental wellness. Kura Kura wants to be a leader in the market for Gen Z mental wellness. Kura Kura's research team is in the process of working on a White Paper to evaluate the mental wellness of Gen Zs in Singapore relative to those in the United States to identify trends and insights that would allow them to develop new features for the app. The company is looking at partnering insurance agencies as they have become more involved in managing mental health.

Ultimately, Kura Kura hopes to get Kura Kura to everyone in Asia and has its sights on expanding to Asian markets such as Vietnam and China, which have expressed interest in the product.

Chapter 9

Drive Ride Buddy (A Digital Journey)

Introduction

While most car purchases from authorized dealers come complete with maintenance services and other value-adds such as breakdown towing, most buyers of parallel-imported and pre-owned cars do not have such privileges. It is common practice for owners of used cars to source for their own after-sales service providers. With a myriad of car servicing and repair centers across Singapore, it is challenging for such owners to find reliable service providers, both in service quality and pricing. Statistics released by the Consumers Association of Singapore (CASE) reveal that the car industry tops its complaints list from 2012 to 2017.[1] Inexperienced car owners are more susceptible to being short-changed by various car servicing workshops that provide sub-standard servicing and overcharged fees. Thomas Tham, a young entrepreneur, recognized this gap and created a tech solution, Drive Ride Buddy (DRB), to tackle this problem.

Founded in 2019, DRB serves as a unified platform to help first-time owners of second-hand vehicles (primarily cars and motorcycles) meet their vehicle servicing needs. DRB is a smartphone-based platform that matches vehicle owners to car repair workshops and other

---

[1] CASE, n.d., Percentage Breakdown of Consumer Complaints, https://www.case.org.sg/consumer_guides_statistics.aspx

service providers. It has features such as a secured built-in payment system, personalized recommendations, transparent pricing, and rating reviews of service providers. The ecosystem approach of DRB ensures that the variety and quality of services on its platform remain high amid a rapidly expanding pool of providers. With the platform business approach, DRB further creates an e-market that extends its services to include sales of motor-vehicle-related accessories.

The Founders

Thomas Tham and Irene Chan co-founded DRB. Thomas has a strong aspiration to create something for himself that would positively impact those around him. His first entrepreneurship encounter was during his National Service days. He started a tutor matchmaking service, which matched students to tutors based on their tutor database and earned commissions from the tutors. This service eventually led to an aggregated tutoring business. However, in 2017, an undisclosed company entered the market with the same business idea, dampening his long-awaited dream of being a first-mover right under his feet.

Later the same year, a friend from his church approached Thomas with an idea involving vehicle workshops. Together, the pair developed Wheels, later known as Drive Ride Buddy. However, despite having some discussions, progress was slow, and the partnership was soon dissolved, and Thomas was back to square one.

Fast forward to 2019, Thomas still had high hopes for the business idea, Drive Ride Buddy, and decided that he did not want to miss out on the opportunity again. Thomas immediately began scouting for members with complementary skills and knowledge to add value to the team. Thankfully, after a few good discussions, DRB was re-launched in 2020.

Vehicle Industry

Singapore has experienced a more than 50% increase in annual vehicle resales in the past decade. The industry faces a high threat of new entrants due to low entry barriers because of the relatively low capital requirements. Furthermore, as DRB is still in its early stage of development, it does not have economies of scale or strong brand loyalty, making it easy for new entrants to enter the market and capture its market share.

Presently, there are few existing competitors in Singapore in terms of online services that compete with the full suite of services of DRB. However, there are several overlaps with the services offered by Automobile Association Singapore (AAS). Unlike DRB, AAS has strong brand loyalty and high quality of services. Buyers are said to have high bargaining power as many car dealerships have existing partnerships with insurance companies and repair workshops, offering them a wide variety of options to choose from. On the other hand, there is relatively low bargaining power of suppliers. Many suppliers of a similar size and low uniqueness of the services and products on offer have little bargaining power.

A Digital Journey

"To empower its users with credible information and services at their fingertips while helping businesses with easy to implement solutions helping to increase business efficiency, value and customer satisfaction." (Drive Ride Buddy, 2021)

DRB has created a platform linking merchants and consumers along the pre-owned vehicle value chain, of which the most crucial activity is car servicing and repair (Figure 1). The platform encourages transactions by improving the transparency of an otherwise opaque environment, from quotations to payment security. DRB has created value for its customers by optimizing the car servicing experience, providing stream-lined car-servicing coordination, lower service prices, and ensuring reliability and accountability for all its users. As a smartphone platform, users can access DRB's services from anywhere with an internet connection and have greater access to a wide variety of service providers through location-based recommendations.

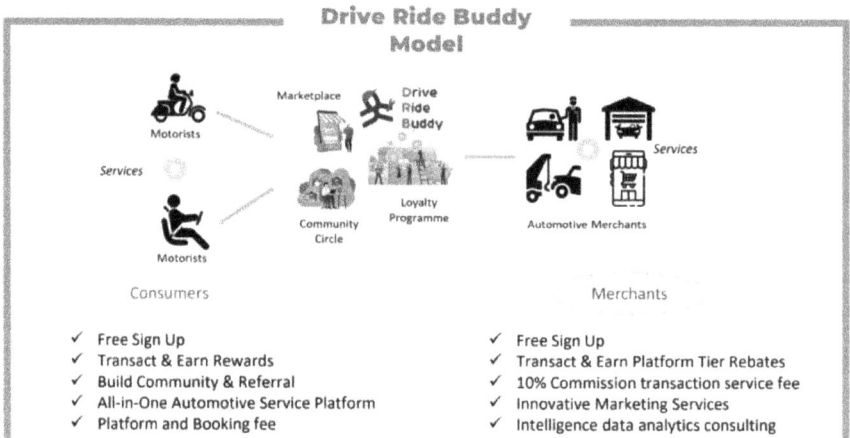

Figure 1:   DRB's Business Model

DRB establishes itself as a platform that guarantees reliable and trustworthy car servicing that removes ambiguities around potential hidden costs. The platform promotes customer/service advocacy with feedback channels to improve its services. As a platform built around a community, DRB has created an ecosystem that allows users to work together to improve the industry. With several service level agreements (SLA) in place, DRB ensures that services rendered by merchants are of high quality.

Another feature that helps DRB set itself apart from competitors is the AI search engine and booking system with a real-time calendar system. This feature makes vehicle servicing convenient and easy as users can personalize their bookings to fit into their schedules. Besides linking users to vehicle servicing providers, the platform has an e-market for service providers to sell parts and accessories. DRB uses this market to engage users with the latest products and provide them with interesting articles on vehicles and other related topics.

A Closer Look at Drive Ride Buddy

Currently, DRB caters particularly to the needs of young consumers, first-time owners of pre-owned vehicles that do not come bundled with insurance and car servicing in their purchase. The core design of DRB aims to solve issues regarding workshop service quality, efficiency, reliability, cost of services, and convenience. The smartphone-based platform features include:

1. Service platform for car servicing, breakdown towing, grooming.
   a. E-Payment
   b. AI search engine with a real-time scheduling system
   c. Market analytics powered by data
   d. Job notifications for merchants
2. Car-valet services.
3. 5-star rating system.
4. E-market for car accessories.
5. New car loan calculator.

Target markets

Merchants play the role of producers in DRB's platform, and they are primarily vehicle (cars and motorcycles) servicing, repair, and paint shops. These merchants are the leading providers of the services to which DRB is offering consumers on their platform. DRB can provide them with greater accessibility to a larger pool of potential customers with an ecosystem approach, helping these service providers raise awareness, build reputation, and increase their base of loyal customers if they consistently perform well.

Additionally, the platform features partner products such as vehicle parts and accessories, allowing these partners to build a strong brand identity while reaching a broader audience via the digital space. Merchants on the DRB platform can use DRB's loyalty program, which offers vouchers for grooming workshops, sanitization, body wrapping, cleaning, and other services (Figure 2).

DRB's product features and offerings can extend beyond cars. Other types of vehicles, including motorcycles or e-bikes, present themselves as a viable feature extension in markets where they are prevalent. The Asian market, which accounts for approximately 80% of global motorcycle demand, heralds it as a predominant mode of transport in some Asian markets, such as Vietnam.

We are Different !

Automotive Loyalty Program	Community Circle*	Marketplace*
• 1st in Singapore	• Sharing of photos & videos	• Sell & Buy
• Earn Points when transact		• Rent & Use
• Gamification Rewards*	• Follow based on interests with other Buddies	• Allow Merchant to Merchant transact (different price)
• Range of category for redemption*		
• Merchants to have Tier Rebates *	• Merchants to promote exclusive discounts	
• Encouraged loyalty and New sales		

Figure 2: DRB's Features

The company has carefully analyzed the various consumer target groups within the DRB platform and settled for individual drivers between 18 to 28 years old, out of two key considerations:

1. This consumer group typically includes new license holders who are first-time vehicle owners. They lack car ownership experience and are worried about going to the wrong service providers.
2. The key features of DRB revolve around new tools in the digital business space. Content engagement, advocacy, crowd-sourced ratings, direct merchant-consumer transactions, location-based recommendations, personalizations, and e-payments are core user experiences delivered through mobile applications. In contrast to the older generation, mobile applications are a great fit for 18 to 28 year-olds.

The team

The company is currently operated by a team composed of Thomas, Irene, and three other co-founders. Thomas and Irene have an IT background with experience in managing IT vendors. Through their experience, they have access to and can leverage on an IT vendor's database with personnel possessing a wide range of skills and knowledge required by the DRB team. The company is currently in talks with a third-party based in Singapore to support its customer services as DRB hopes to provide 24/7 customer support for its users. Thomas is setting up an internal technical team to provide in-house technical support and advice for its users.

Most of the company's software developers in its operational team are outsourced to a programming service provider in India. The current team working for DRB has been with the company for over a year. DRB is working toward obtaining the funding and resources to hire an in-house development team but will continue working with third parties to meet its maintenance services.

Revenue & Cost Models

Revenue and cost drivers

The financing model of the DRB platform is based on commissions charged to producers for all transactions performed through the platform. During the development stage, most of the company's funds are spent on platform development paid to its third-party service developers in India. Staffing is the next major cost item to the company.

Impact of COVID-19

Although COVID-19 has had an enormous impact on the economy and many industries, DRB has managed to identify several opportunities arising from the pandemic and leveraged them. One such opportunity is the adoption and recognition of the need for digitalized processes. With more people working from home and businesses having to cut down physical operations, there has been an increase in the demand for digital solutions. The pandemic has also given DRB more time to reflect on its business plan and develop a clear course of action.

As a start-up company, research plays a vital role in identifying the direction it should be heading and the kind of services wanted by potential customers. However, the pandemic has created many challenges for the company as many existing commitments have been halted. For example, the pandemic has made it harder for DRB to garner constructive feedback from focus groups. DRB overcomes this challenge by using online surveys and social media to continue receiving feedback and suggestions from the public.

Moving Forward

Onboarding of vendors

Currently, DRB has begun onboarding new vendors with the focus on ensuring they can commit to a non-cancellation booking scheme. The agreements signed by onboarded vendors are non-exclusive, thus not restricting them from extending their services to other business partners. Discussions are underway between DRB and selected local dealers for certain brands of products to be sold at preferential rates exclusively on DRB's platform.

Customer loyalty system

DRB is developing a loyalty program to increase customer stickiness while amplifying the company's branding through partnerships. Customers will be awarded points for purchases and recommendations to the platform that can be used for service and product redemption within three months. Consumers can get cashback benefits and redeem vouchers for achieving various targeted expenditure amounts.

A gamification element on the platform is in the works to generate a sense of active involvement beyond the mere use of its functions. Challenges and daily tasks such as charity programs, community involvement, long-distance mileage, and promotional event challenges are created for users to participate and complete in exchange for virtual badges or achievements. Fostering community participation on the platform into social and charitable causes is in line with DRB's Corporate Social Responsibility (CSR) values. Such values would transcend beyond short-term business development and have a lasting impact as a long-term core competency of DRB that projects a positive image beyond the limits of its target market.

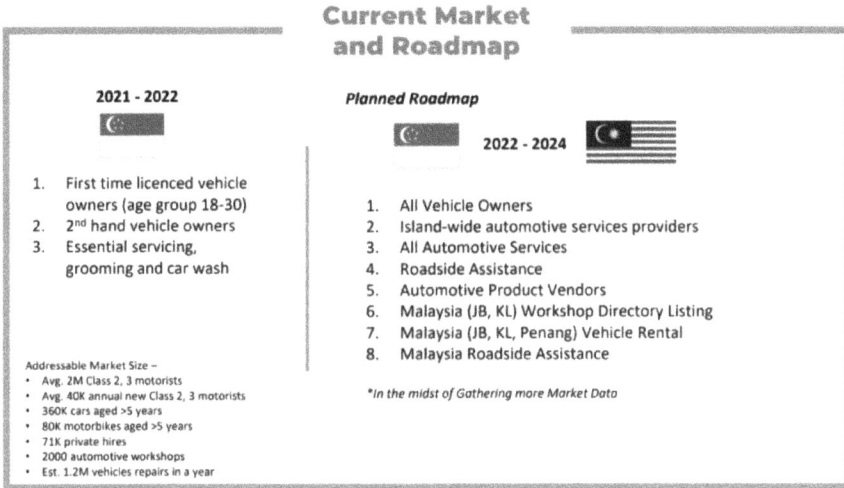

Current Market and Roadmap

2021 - 2022

1. First time licenced vehicle owners (age group 18-30)
2. 2nd hand vehicle owners
3. Essential servicing, grooming and car wash

Addressable Market Size –
- Avg. 2M Class 2, 3 motorists
- Avg. 40K annual new Class 2, 3 motorists
- 360K cars aged >5 years
- 80K motorbikes aged >5 years
- 71K private hires
- 2000 automotive workshops
- Est. 1.2M vehicles repairs in a year

Planned Roadmap

2022 - 2024

1. All Vehicle Owners
2. Island-wide automotive services providers
3. All Automotive Services
4. Roadside Assistance
5. Automotive Product Vendors
6. Malaysia (JB, KL) Workshop Directory Listing
7. Malaysia (JB, KL, Penang) Vehicle Rental
8. Malaysia Roadside Assistance

In the midst of Gathering more Market Data

Figure 3:   DRB's roadmap

Expansion Into Malaysia

DRB plans to expand into Malaysia, starting with the states of Johor and Perak, by reaching out to workshops there and replicating its Singapore merchant reach-out programs. Its operations in Malaysia are focused primarily on workshop listings instead of roadside recovery services. Besides addressing staffing matters and onboarding of local merchants, DRB has shifted its focus to improving its local marketing campaigns and placed a greater emphasis on motorcyclists (Figure 3).

To fast-track their expansion into Malaysia, DRB has initiated talks with strategic partners. As discussions and negotiations are still at their initial stage, there are currently no concrete plans of the nature of such a venture/partnership. DRB hopes to form a symbiotic relationship that would allow them to tap into the Malaysian merchants' network and for strategic partners to likewise tap into Singapore via DRB, giving both parties the impetus to fast-track their international growth.

Index